IN THE
BEGINNING

Life Lessons From Genesis

IN THE
BEGINNING

Life Lessons From Genesis

JUSTIN ROGERS

GOSPEL
ADVOCATE

A TRUSTED NAME SINCE 1855

Published by Gospel Advocate Co.
1006 Elm Hill Pike, Nashville, TN 37210
www.gospeladvocate.com

ISBN: 978-0-89225-657-0

TABLE OF CONTENTS

Foreword

Christians need a solid understanding of the book of Genesis, for Genesis provides a foundation on which the whole biblical narrative rests. Historically, much error has entered the church when this foundation has been ignored or denied.

Jesus and His apostles often placed their teachings squarely within the framework of the Genesis narrative, and without an understanding of Genesis, much New Testament teaching would be incomprehensible. The apostle Paul's teaching of justification by faith, for example, presupposes a familiarity with the story of Abraham, and his explanation of gender roles in the church rests on a knowledge of the account of Adam and Eve. A thorough knowledge of Genesis shines a light on the rest of Scripture.

For this reason, I am thankful Justin Rogers has provided the brotherhood this excellent study.

I first met Justin some years ago at the Freed-Hardeman University Lectures. He was selling books in a display at the southwest corner of Bader Gymnasium. We struck up a conversation, which resumed annually, with my return to Henderson each February for the lectures. By the time Justin had completed his studies at FHU, we had become friends, and he was contributing articles regularly for the *Gospel Advocate*.

Justin continued his education, earning his doctorate from Hebrew Union College. A talented linguist, he is well-regarded by peers in his field of study. Attaining his degree, Justin returned to FHU as a professor of Bible.

This depth of study and academic preparation give Justin standing to write this book. Anyone can slap words on paper, and in this age of self-publishing many do so. But not everyone should presume to foist their views on the brotherhood. At the Gospel Advocate Company, we look for qualified authors to edify the Lord's people.

Beyond academic excellence, Justin brings to his writing the perspective of a man steeped in church work. Growing up in a preacher's home, he, along with his family, made the local congregation their business. Justin continues to serve as an evangelist in local work in addition to his university position. This commitment to serve God's people gives Justin's writing a practical accessibility so often lacking in purely academic work. As a simple Midwestern preacher, I appreciate the way Justin has taken the depth of his scholarship and presented it in a way all can understand. This book is designed to be read by every member of the Lord's church – equally suited for classroom use and for private study.

I commend this book to the brotherhood because Justin is my friend and is a part of the Gospel Advocate family of writers. I commend this book because of Justin's keen mind and academic preparation. I commend this book because of Justin's willingness to stay in the front line of the Lord's work, preaching for a congregation of God's people. All of these good things, however, would not matter if the most-important thing were not in place.

Justin Rogers is a man of faith. He believes the Bible as the Word of God. His confidence in the inerrancy and authority of Scripture permeates everything Justin writes and fills his words with spiritual power. You, also, will be empowered if you read this book and become better acquainted with what God has said to us in the book of Genesis. For this reason, beyond everything else, I commend this book to you.

Gregory Alan Tidwell
Editor, *Gospel Advocate*

Preface

The book of Genesis has long been a battleground between believers and skeptics. But a shift has occurred over the last few decades. Now more and more believers are suggesting that less and less of Genesis is reliable. Some see the creation account as a mere poem rather than a historical record (note how the 2011 edition of the New International Version sets Genesis 1 in poetic type). Some think that the historical existence of Adam and Eve is irrelevant to people of faith (note Greg Boyd's views on the historical Adam). Many believe that the flood account is merely borrowed from other deluge myths, such as the *Epic of Gilgamesh*.

It seems that many in our world wish to sit over the book of Genesis in judgment of what is right and wrong, of what is historical and what is mythological. The book you are now reading is not intended to counter the critics. A thorough defense of Genesis may be appropriate, but I wish to be more positive in this book. I assume that the book of Genesis is a historical document on which we can base our faith. Jesus treated Genesis as history as did the apostles (Mark 10:6-8; Luke 17:26-27; Romans 4:1-25; 2 Peter 2: 4-9; 1 John 3:12). Throughout the book we learn of men and women who submit their lives in service to God. Ultimately, each of these faithful figures is successful. Indeed, "the eyes of the LORD are on the righteous, And His ears are open to their prayers; but the face of the LORD is against those who do evil" (1 Peter 3:12).

Acknowledgements

A number of people have had a hand in the production of this book. Billy Smith assigned me to teach Genesis during my first year at Freed-Hardeman University and every year since. Isaac Bourne read the earliest versions of the manuscript, and made invaluable comments. The good brethren at Christian Chapel Church of Christ in Wildersville, Tenn., listened patiently to numerous iterations of the material in their oral form.

Dennis Loyd and the Gospel Advocate staff have kindly steered me away from a number of errors and made vast improvements to the work as a whole. Greg Tidwell deserves special mention, without whose energy and encouragement the current product would never have seen the light of day.

Finally, to my wife, Ashli, and to my children, Caleb and Chelsea: thank you.

1

ORIGINS
OF THE
CREATOR
Genesis 1:1

"God is dead," wrote the famous German philosopher Friedrich Nietzsche in 1882.[1] This statement is often used to shock people into believing that religion is silly. Those who believe in a god – any god – are perceived to be weak-minded, uneducated and superstitious. Christians are even worse! They attempt to brainwash people into believing that a mysterious creature, half-God and half-man, entered the world, performed miracles, was murdered and came back to life. This God-man then ascended into the clouds and vanished. Many philosophers and scientists regard the biblical stories as nonsense, purporting that these things did not happen because they *cannot* happen.

God and Our Culture

Skepticism about the existence of God abounds in our culture. Christians often blame this skepticism on the prevalence of evolutionary biology in our public school systems. But the problem is much larger and more complex than what is taught in public school. Atheism is no longer merely a philosophical position. It has become a lifestyle. We might refer to this position as "practical atheism." Although many Americans still believe in God, He no longer makes a difference in how they live.

Our culture has no need for God because intellectual arrogance rules the day.

> **Atheism is no longer merely a philosophical position. It has become a lifestyle.**

In education, "We are the smartest people ever!" In business, "We are the wealthiest people ever!" In politics, "We live in the greatest country ever!" As a people, we aim at more knowledge, more money, more power ... and the story continues with each succeeding generation. Is this not the "American dream"? But if the American dream is a fierce determination to succeed by virtue of myself, haven't I missed something? Where do I learn to submit? When do I learn to serve?

Our personal and societal success has blinded many of us from recognizing that our greatest spiritual triumphs are often won in our worst moments of despair. When we are broken and confused, when we are exhausted and alone, when we recognize our own limitations and long for something (or someone) greater than ourselves – only then are we prepared to be molded by God. Then we are willing to submit. Then we are willing to serve. This process of being shaped and molded begins with the Bible itself – the revelation of God's will.

Where do I learn to submit? When do I learn to serve?

The Bible claims that God is responsible for everything around us. He created the world. He revealed to people how He wants them to live. And, yes, God sent His Son – completely human, yet completely divine – to this earth. To this God we are to submit. But where did God come from? Has He just always been? Was He created? Do we need Him?

Where Did God Come From?

This question has been asked for centuries, but the question itself reflects a simplistic view of things. For example, almost everything we use on a daily basis has a traceable origin. Our breakfast cereal begins as grain in a field. Our books begin as trees in a forest, but not everything we experience can be traced so easily.

Elements of the Earth

Where does the wind come from? Scientists might say, "Atmospheric pressures lead nitrogen, oxygen and water molecules to move from high pressure areas to low pressure areas ... blah, blah, blah." But this is not really an answer. What is the *origin* of the wind? Most scientists would answer, "It's just always been here – it is part of the earth's atmosphere." Jesus Himself verified this fact when He said, "The wind blows where it wishes, and you hear the sound of it, but cannot tell where it comes from and where it goes" (John 3:8).

Where does water come from? Scientists may tell us, "Evaporation leads to condensation, condensation leads to precipitation, and precipitation leads to collection." This is the water cycle. But the water cycle is simply an explanation of how water is recycled by the earth. What is the *origin* of water? "Well," scientists tell us, "it's always been here."

So we can see that there are elements on this earth that, even scientists must acknowledge, have always been here. Why is it that nonbelievers can agree that we cannot explain the origin of the wind or water, but they ridicule us when we say the same thing about the origin of God? In fact, God *has* always been. And if God was "in the beginning," as the Bible says, then God must be the source of the wind and water. These things actually *do* have a beginning. God created them (Genesis 1:6-10).

> **Why is it that nonbelievers can agree that we cannot explain the origin of the wind or water, but they ridicule us when we say the same thing about the origin of God?**

The Nature of Life

Beyond the earthly examples of elements that have always been, we can further explain that God was "in the beginning" by the nature of life itself. The fact that life exists on earth is evidence of a living Creator. Rocks and dirt do not, by themselves, produce life.[2] By simple logic, we can believe that a living Creator could create things that are both living (like animals) and non-living (like water, wind, rocks and dirt). But a non-living creator (like rocks or crystals – as imagined by atheists) could never create life. Let us illustrate this principle.

The Bible affirms that each living thing produces "after its kind." This is true of both plants (Genesis 1:11-12) and animals (vv. 21, 24-25). The after-its-kind principle can be observed in nature. Pine cones do not produce apple trees. Although pine trees and apple trees are both classified as trees, one does not produce the other. The same is true of animals. Gorillas do not give birth to chickens. All trees share certain characteristics, such as synthesis of nutrients from the soil and sunlight. All animals share certain qualities, such as breathing and digestion of food. Despite these similarities, living things produce exclusively after their own kind.

Although all intelligent people acknowledge this principle in the case of pine trees and gorillas, some scientists and philosophers attempt to reverse the principle when it comes to the origins of plant and animal life. They say that rocks and dirt produced plants and animals. So which is more logical? To believe that rocks and dirt (non-living entities) produced plants and animals (living entities) or that a living Creator produced both? But who is this Creator? What can we know about Him?

Who Is God?

The Bible tells us about God. It tells of God's love (1 John 4:8); it tells of God's Son and His church (Matthew 16:18); and it tells of God's desire that all people be saved (1 Timothy 2:4). The Bible offers the most complete picture of who God is. But we can know certain things about God simply by looking at His creation.

What Nature Teaches About God

Speaking of God, Paul wrote, "For since the creation of the world His invisible attributes are clearly seen, being understood by the things that are made, even His eternal power and Godhead, so that they are without excuse" (Romans 1:20). Paul affirmed paradoxically that we can clearly see the invisible aspects of God in the visible world. These invisible aspects include God's power, which is always evident in His creation.

God never loses power. Every super hero has a weakness. Superman's power weakens when he is around kryptonite. Iron Man is an ordinary man without his robotic suit. But the God who created the world has lost none of His power since the beginning of time. The power of hurricanes, volcanos and tornadoes astonishes us. Even with the best of technology, we cannot control these natural disasters. And God created them.

The God who created the world has lost none of His power since the beginning of time.

This leads us to a principle of creation: Creation can be no greater than its creator. Nature itself teaches this lesson. If I make a chair out of wood, I am greater than the chair because I made it. If you assemble a clock out of thousands of tiny parts, you are greater than the clock because you put it together. The clock is a pile of parts on its own, incapable of keeping time. The chair is a pile of wood on its own. The creator gives purpose and value to creation. If everything was created by God, then God is necessarily greater than everything created – including the most powerful natural events such as tornadoes and hurricanes.

So we can see from nature that God does exist and that He is powerful. But the Bible informs us about God in greater detail. Without the Bible, we would not know about God's rules for life. We would not know about God's Son, who died for us. We would not know about the church that Jesus died to establish. Our portrait of God may have an outline in nature, but it is painted in full color throughout the Bible.

> **Our portrait of God may have an outline in nature, but it is painted in full color throughout the Bible.**

God in the Bible

The God who created the world in the beginning (Genesis 1:1; 2:4) is the same God who rescued Israel from Egyptian slavery (Exodus 20:2). This God gave the Law of Moses (40:1ff.; Leviticus 1:1ff.; Numbers 1:1ff.). This God inspired Moses and others to predict the coming of Jesus Christ (Deuteronomy 18:15-19; Isaiah 7:14; Micah 5:2). This God promised to establish His kingdom on the earth (Daniel 2:44; 7:14). This God raised Jesus from the dead (Acts 2:24; 13:30; 1 Corinthians 6:14; Galatians 1:1). Some may doubt Him; others reject Him. But the God of creation is the God of the crucifixion, and the God of the crucifixion is the God of salvation and judgment.

In the Bible we learn that this same God wishes to communicate with man (Hebrews 1:1-2) and that He has a plan of redemption that was in motion "before the foundation of the world" (Ephesians 1:4). We further learn that God has established a plan of salvation whereby we can be saved (Acts 2:38; 1 Peter 3:21). The Creator of the universe is both powerful and loving. He has established the world in which we live, and He has offered us salvation from the sins of that world. Finally, His Son has prepared a place of rest for us at the end of our lives (John 14:1-3; 1 Peter 1:4).

The Names of God

The two primary names for God in the Old Testament are "God" and "Lord." The name "God" indicates that the Creator is a divine being – spiritual in nature and in no way human. The name "Lord" indicates God's eternal existence. God made this part of His nature clear in Exodus 3:14: "And God said to Moses, 'I AM WHO I AM.' And He said, 'Thus you shall say to the children of Israel, "I AM has sent me to you."'" Jesus made a similar statement when He said, "Most assuredly, I say to you, before Abraham was, I AM" (John 8:58).

Both of these passages make for difficult English translation, but the meaning is clear. Both the LORD and Jesus Christ have always existed. They had no beginning, nor will They have an end. They are truly eternal. They, along with the Holy Spirit, are the only beings who have always existed. No matter what scientists and philosophers may say, both nature and common sense justify the belief in a Creator. The fourth word of the Bible introduces us to that Creator, and the rest of Scripture is commentary.

> **Both the LORD and Jesus Christ have always existed. They had no beginning, nor will They have an end.**

Conclusion

God is not dead, as Nietzsche proclaimed. He was alive before the beginning (Exodus 3:14; John 8:58), and He will remain at the end (Revelation 21:6). Atheists may laugh at the fourth word of the Bible, calling the idea of God foolish. Evolutionists may disagree with the fifth word of the Bible, calling creation a hoax. But for those of us who seek to understand who this God is and where He came from, the first verse of the Bible is just the beginning of the journey.

Discussion Questions

1. Discuss the earthly elements of wind and water. How do these help us understand and explain the origin of God?

2. How does Romans 1:20 relate to our understanding of God from nature?

3. Discuss the after-its-kind principle. How does it apply to creation?

4. Name some of the facts we learn about God only from the Bible.

2

THE BAGGAGE
OF
BIBLICAL CREATION
Genesis 1-2

Jason opened his science textbook to read the words, "Almost all scientists in the world believe that life developed through evolution." After reading these words, Jason became confused. He had always been taught that God created all forms of life. But God is not necessary in the evolutionary system. In fact, many scientists do not believe in God at all.

Jason then asked his teacher how evolution began, thinking perhaps she would help him understand how God fit in. His teacher replied, "We do not know *how* evolution began; we know only *that* it began. And no serious scientist," she continued, "believes that God exists."

The opening chapter of the Bible is a straightforward record of facts.

Jason was crushed. He respected his teacher and valued her opinions. But how could his church be so wrong about something so important? How could so many scientists and science teachers believe in evolution? The Bible says that "God created the heavens and the earth" (Genesis 1:1).

The opening chapter of the Bible is a straightforward record of facts. There is no indication that life evolved. It issues no challenge to alternate theories of creation. Nevertheless, modern scientists, scholars and even some "Christians" have thrust onto the book of Genesis ideas that are not there. They tell us that evolution is common sense. But is it?

Barriers to Belief in Evolution
Evolution is often treated as fact, and biblical creation, as foolishness.

But many philosophers and scientists ignore very obvious problems with evolution. At the same time, they ignore very obvious merits of biblical creation. There are, in fact, several reasons to doubt evolution and accept biblical creation.

Biblical Creation Affirms the Origin of Matter

Many atheistic scientists believe that matter is eternal. Christians may not be able to explain the concept of an eternal Creator, but the concept of eternal matter is even more difficult to explain. This is true especially when we are told that eternal matter is constantly in the process of evolving into something else. Others suggest that matter had a beginning but not with God. Whether this happened as a result of a pre-historic cosmic explosion such as the "Big Bang," no one can agree. But eternal matter, we are told, is still in a constant state of change.

Others suggest that matter had a beginning but not with God.

The Bible affirms that the God of Scripture, however, created matter (Ephesians 3:9; Revelation 4:11). Nothing had its origin outside of His creative will and complete control. And Jesus, functioning as the Word, was the agent through whom everything came into existence, for "without Him nothing was made that was made" (John 1:3). Further, the Bible affirms that God, unlike the matter imagined by the atheistic evolutionist, does not change: "For I am the LORD, I do not change" (Malachi 3:6). The God of the Bible had no beginning or end (Psalm 90:2). His eternality was never changed or lessened in creation. While matter as imagined by evolutionists is eternal and subject to constant change, the biblical God of creation is the same as the God of eternity.

Biblical Creation Explains the Origin of Life

Scientists who believe in evolution cannot explain how life came from non-life. They simply *assume* that it must have happened because there are living beings. But there is a problem. If non-living matter created living organisms "in the beginning," then we should see a similar thing happening today. We do not. Scientists can "grow" living organisms in labs. They can even produce human beings by artificially fertilizing eggs. But they cannot take a pile of dirt and produce anything alive. They must begin with life to produce life. How is it that the universe created life from non-life only once and never again? What evolutionists *cannot* answer, creationists can: Life came into existence when it was created by a living God.

Biblical Creation Explains the Origin of Intelligence

Not all life functions the same way. Plants are alive, but they do not have brains. Dogs have brains, but they do not read books. Human intelligence is clearly the highest form of intelligence. Evolutionists want us to believe that ignorance produced intelligence. Life began with brainless organisms that had no self-awareness and evolved into animals with brains and self-awareness. Biblical creation teaches us the opposite idea. God is the highest form of intelligence. He created plants with life but not with intelligence. He created animals with limited intelligence. Finally, he created human beings with the greatest intellect in the created universe. Does it make more sense to say that simple, unintelligent organisms produced complex, intelligent ones, or is it better to believe that an intelligent God created all beings?

> Evolutionists feel certain that there was no intelligent designer. But without scientific proof, how can they be so certain?

Evolution Requires More Faith Than Biblical Creation

Evolutionary theorists will often smugly brush off biblical creationists as fundamentalists with nothing to prove their ideas. "Scientific inquiry," they say, "must proceed along with evidence, not by blind faith." But evolutionary theory actually requires a great deal of faith. Can any scientist or philosopher explain *how* life began and *how* it got to earth? Can any scientist or philosopher explain how intelligence began? Evolutionists feel certain that there was no intelligent designer. But without scientific proof, how can they be so certain? Faith.

Belief in Biblical Creation

So what evidence do we have that a loving God is responsible for the world? We can see in the universe the evidence of God's design.

God Designed the Universe

Have you ever looked under the hood of your car? There are many parts: a radiator, a battery, tanks for various fluids, and so on. It is obvious to all of us that these parts are essential for the operation of our cars. Now imagine someone told you that there was a tornado in a car factory, and all the auto parts went flying and spinning through the air. Then they all landed perfectly in place so that the hundreds of auto parts that make up a car were accidentally fitted together perfectly. Total nonsense, right? Yet this is exactly what many scientists tell us happened in the creation of the universe. It was all a happy accident.

Let's imagine something less complex. T-shirts are generally woven together from cotton or other fabrics. Imagine that someone told you a tractor trailer hauling cotton wrecked on the side of the road and tons of cotton went flying through the air. A truck went speeding by and hit that cloud of cotton, ripping it into shreds. Then those shreds, as they floated from the air to the ground, began to bind to one another and weave themselves together into hundreds of white T-shirts before safely landing in neat stacks. Ridiculous? This kind of idea is precisely what many of the "finest" scientific minds are presenting to college students in some of the country's universities.

> **Why is the earth tilted slightly less than 23.5 degrees? ... Someone created it this way.**

The truth is this: We know that T-shirts and cars were put together by *someone*. We know this because their constituent parts fit together too well for them to have been made by accident. The complexity of the universe teaches us the same lesson. Why do we experience winter, spring, summer and fall? Why is the earth tilted slightly less than 23.5 degrees? Why does the earth make a full rotation every 24 hours? Evolutionists answer, "It's all an accident." But anyone with common sense would conclude that these things are too precise to be an accident. Someone must have created them this way. The Bible in fact exclaims: "The heavens declare the glory of God; and the firmament shows His handiwork" (Psalm 19:1).

What About the Problem of Evil?

Many people object to the idea of a loving Creator because evil is in the world. The Bible teaches that God is good (Psalm 73:1; Micah 6:8; Mark 10:18; 3 John 11). The Bible also teaches that God is in control of the universe and everything in it (Psalm 24:1; Daniel 4:25; 1 Corinthians 10:26). If this is the case, then why does God allow earthquakes, hurricanes, tornadoes and other disasters that take the lives of thousands of innocent people? Why does God allow murder, adultery, child abuse and other forms of evil? If God is powerful enough to stop evil in our world, why does evil exist?

One way to explain the existence of evil in the world is to relate evil to the problem of sin. God created human beings with the ability to choose right and wrong. The temptation of Eve in Genesis 3 makes no sense unless Eve was actually free to choose whether to eat the fruit. God did not snatch the forbidden fruit from Eve's grasp and play "keep-away." He allowed both Eve and Adam to *choose* to sin. Eve and Adam chose poorly.

If God is powerful enough to stop evil in our world, why does evil exist?

Sometimes human beings make poor choices. Someone who engages in sex before marriage makes a poor, ungodly decision. Someone who allows anger to drive him or her to murder or to abuse another person makes a poor decision. But everyone is free to choose. This means that we are also free to choose good.

God has given us instructions to follow. If we are willing to follow these instructions, we demonstrate our love for God (John 14:15), and we are declared faithful (Revelation 2:10). God will never stop us from making a bad decision. He will, however, help us escape sin (1 Corinthians 10:13). Some of the evil in the world can be explained by the poor decisions of man.

What about natural disasters? God is in control of the weather (Psalm 148:8; Zechariah 14:17; Matthew 8:27). This means that God should stop natural disasters from occurring, right? After all, it isn't fair for a hurricane or a wildfire to kill hundreds or thousands of innocent people, is it?

We must recognize that natural disasters are an essential part of nature. Wildfires sometimes burn throughout the western U.S., restoring vital nutrients to the soil so that forest debris can be cleared for new growth. Hurricanes serve at least two natural purposes. In the first place, they serve to clear heat and moisture from the equator. This is why we experience hurricane season. Only at certain times of the year does the area around the equator become warm enough for hurricanes to form. Second, hurricanes serve to bring necessary rain and moisture to certain parts of the world. More than half of Japan's annual rainfall, for example, comes as a result of hurricanes in the ocean. We tend to focus purely on the human toll and conclude that fires and hurricanes are evil. In fact, they are necessary for the earth's climate system.

We tend to focus purely on the human toll and conclude that fires and hurricanes are evil.

Whenever philosophers or scientists raise objections to biblical creation, such as the problem of evil, we can answer these questions by understanding that God created the entire universe to work together for the benefit of the whole. By focusing only on a small part of God's creation, such as the loss of life in a storm or earthquake, one is guilty of ignoring the natural benefits to other parts of God's creation. A book is not considered a great work of literature because of a single sentence, nor is a painting praised because of a single color. God's creation should be understood by considering the whole and never by focusing only on a small part.

Conclusion

Evolution is not a fact. It is a theory of origins – a theory, we may add, full of problems and contradictions. Biblical creation is simple and direct. Biblical creation is biblically justified and logically coherent. The same cannot be said for evolution. The idea of biblical creation answers the most difficult questions, which evolution cannot answer. For anyone who wishes to follow the Scriptures and respect the evidence placed in the world around us, the only possible conclusion is that our world was designed and created by a loving God.

Discussion Questions

1. How is the God of the Bible superior to matter?

2. What problem does the existence of life present to evolutionists? How can biblical creation explain this problem?

3. What evidence is there for design in the universe? Think of examples not used in this book.

4. Why do many atheists consider evil a problem? How can we answer these objections?

A SNAKE
IN THE
GARDEN OF GOD
Genesis 3

"Sticks and stones may break my bones, but words will never hurt me." This saying is well-known to most children, but it is wrong. Words can hurt us deeply. When a friend embarrasses us with a Facebook post or when a relative ridicules us behind our backs, he or she is only speaking or typing words. But those words definitely affect our relationships.

Words are powerful. The book of Proverbs warns us, "Death and life are in the power of the tongue, and those who love it will eat its fruit" (Proverbs 18:21). Adam and Eve most certainly ate the fruit. They accepted whatever the snake told them. Although he spoke only 26 Hebrew words, the snake was so persuasive that both Adam and Eve sinned against God and were banished from Paradise forever.

The temptation of Adam and Eve in Genesis 3 is a specific historical event. But the methods of temptation used by the snake are typical of all temptation. We can learn several lessons about temptation from this passage.

The Devil's Shell Game

Imagine a magician. The magician places a pea under one of three shells and begins to shift the shells quickly. He then asks, "Who knows where the pea is?" There is a good chance that the shells were moved too quickly for us to know for sure. So someone guesses that the pea is under the third shell. Wrong. Another person guesses the pea is under the first shell. Wrong again. The pea must be under the second shell, right? Nope. What we failed to notice was that while the magician was shifting the shells from one place to another, he had discreetly slid the pea into his hand. We were deceived because our attention was focused in the wrong place.

Satan works in a similar way. He always attempts to confuse us by substituting what isn't important for what really is. Notice how he handled Eve. He asked, "Has God indeed said, 'You shall not eat of every tree of the garden'?" (Genesis 3:1). We cannot know how many fruit trees were in the Garden of Eden. But the number must have been in the dozens or even hundreds. Eve could have eaten the fruit of every other tree and remained in the garden forever. But Satan played a shell game. He confused Eve by focusing her attention on the one and only tree that was forbidden to her. The lesson for us today goes far beyond fruit trees.

Satan always attempts to confuse us by substituting what isn't important for what really is.

A key to satisfaction in life is to "be content with such things as you have" (Hebrews 13:5). The sin of covetousness is simply valuing what you do not possess above what you do possess. Whether the tempter focuses our attention on the nicest automobile, the newest smartphone, or a piece of fruit hanging in a tree, the process is always the same. He wants our minds to be consumed with all the material possessions we do not have. Looking at our modern world, we can see how successful the devil has become. But people of God should be better than that.

We should recognize that everything we possess is a gift from God (Ecclesiastes 5:19; James 1:17). We should be grateful for the things we do have and ignore the things we do not possess. Paul instructed Timothy: "For we brought nothing into this world, and it is certain we can carry nothing out. And having food and clothing, with these we shall be content" (1 Timothy 6:7-8). If Eve had been content with what God had already provided, she never would have sinned.

The Devil's Game of Lies

After the snake was successful in directing Eve's attention to the tree, he then directly contradicted God's command. He stated, "You will not surely die" (Genesis 3:4). To make sure Eve did not immediately object to this obvious contradiction of God's word, the snake continued, "For God knows that in the day you eat of it your eyes will be opened, and you will be like God, knowing good and evil" (v. 5). Notice that the snake told a truth (knowing good and evil), a half-truth (you will be like God), and a lie (you will not die).

Not every temptation is trans-

A key to satisfaction in life is to "be content with such things as you have" (Hebrews 13:5). If Eve had been content with what God had already provided, she never would have sinned.

parent. Sometimes the devil is capable of offering some very good and appropriate things. At the temptation of Jesus, the devil even quoted the Bible (Matthew 4:6). But some very good ideas can lead us into some very bad places. When I was in high school, I wanted to attend a tournament basketball game in Memphis, Tenn. We can all agree that nothing is wrong with that. But the game was being played in an unsafe neighborhood. I did not attend the basketball game. The negative possibilities outweighed the positive.

In Eve's case, there was certainly nothing wrong with the desire to be like God. The Bible actually commands it in other places (Leviticus 19:2; Matthew 5:48). But Eve was unable to see through the immediate situation. She did not consider human innocence as a gift from God. The ability to see through one's immediate circumstances is called *perspective*.

In order to have perspective in the midst of temptation, ask yourself these questions:

(1) Is there anything wrong with this? Eve perhaps initially asked this question because she quoted God (Genesis 3:2-3). But she was soon shaken from her foundation by the deception of the snake. If we answer yes to the first question, we should stop immediately. If something is wrong, we cannot be involved in it.

(2) Where might this decision lead? If an accountant is asked to shift some numbers around to maximize his company's profits, the short-term benefits may be great, but the long-term consequences could be tragic. Asking the second question allows us to prepare for potential problems and to consider the consequences of bad decisions. Eve knew the consequences of sin. God had already warned her: "In the day that

you eat of it you shall surely die" (Genesis 2:17). Unfortunately, her desire for the fruit outweighed her fear of the consequences.

(3) Where is my escape route? Firemen are instructed to mark escape routes when they enter a burning building. They understand the danger in their jobs and the necessity of getting out alive. We too should understand the dangers of sin and keep aware of the possibilities of escape. The Bible comforts us with the knowledge that God "will not allow you to be tempted beyond what you are able [to bear], but with the temptation will also make the way of escape, that you may be able to bear it" (1 Corinthians 10:13). None of us has to sin. None of us is forced to do anything. There is always an escape route, preventing us from falling victim to temptation. Eve could have refused the fruit, but she chose not to. The history of the world hinged on a piece of fruit.

> **None of us has to sin. None of us is forced to do anything. There is always an escape route.**

The Devil's Blame Game

"The devil made me do it." People make this statement when they want to deflect responsibility, but the truth is that we are responsible for our actions. If a team performs well, the coach receives credit and keeps his job. If a team constantly loses, the coach receives blame and will eventually lose his job. In either case, the coach is held responsible. Often, however, coaches will blame others. They may complain about lousy players or poor effort. They may complain about the athletic director. But taking responsibility is a sign of maturity. Micah wrote, "I will bear the indignation of the LORD, because I have sinned against Him" (7:9). Micah understood that he was guilty and would suffer as a result.

In Genesis 3, both Eve and Adam disobeyed God. The Bible focuses attention on Eve because the serpent spoke to her. But Adam was present throughout the entire temptation (Genesis 3:6). He could have (and should have) stopped the temptation. But he did not. When God confronted Adam with his sin, Adam blamed his wife. He exclaimed, "The woman whom You gave to be with me, she gave me of the tree, and I ate" (v. 12). Adam was willing not only to blame his wife, but

also to implicitly blame God – "*You* gave her to me!" But the blame
game did not work. Adam was cursed. He was held responsible.

Eve likewise attempted to shift the blame. She protested, "The serpent deceived me, and I ate" (Genesis 3:13). Adam was not deceived.
He disobeyed God directly. Eve, however, fell as a result of deception
(1 Timothy 2:14). The snake merely planted the idea in the mind
of Eve. She chose to act upon it. Just as her husband, Eve too was
cursed. She was held responsible.

The Devil's Deathblow

After detailing the curses against Adam and Eve, God turned to the
snake and declared: "And I will put enmity between you and the woman,
and between your seed and her Seed; He shall bruise your head, and
you shall bruise His heel" (Genesis 3:15). This passage was read in both
the ancient Jewish sources in reference to the **We are all similar**
Messiah and in ancient Christian sources in **to Adam and Eve.**
reference to Jesus.[1] The snake (understood as **We sin.**
the devil) would attempt to crush the head of
God's Christ but would succeed only in bruising His heel. The Christ,
then, would deliver a deathblow to the head of the devil.

The curse of the snake reveals a very important lesson: Even in
the midst of sin, God is working at redemption. The term "redeem"
means "to buy back." Although Adam and Eve sinned against God
and enslaved themselves to sin, God was already working on a plan
to buy them back with the blood of His Son (cf. 1 John 1:7). He set
in motion this plan of salvation before the foundation of the world
(Ephesians 1:4; Revelation 13:8).

We are all similar to Adam and Eve. We sin. We often fall short of
what God wants for us. But we all have opportunity for redemption
(John 3:16). We need only to recognize our own faults and appeal
to God for a good conscience (1 Peter 3:21).

Conclusion

The Bible assures us that "all have sinned and fall short of the glory
of God" (Romans 3:23). All humans are victims of Satan's temptation. But when we find ourselves down, facing adversity, we can

take comfort in the fact that God is working for us. We can observe the way the devil operates, and we can avoid his schemes (2 Corinthians 2:11). Adam and Eve were tempted with the same schemes that you and I face today. Knowing those schemes and keeping our perspective will enable us to "be sober, be vigilant; because [our] adversary the devil walks about like a roaring lion, seeking whom he may devour" (1 Peter 5:8).

Discussion Questions

1. List some ways the devil attempts to shift our focus from what is important. How can we avoid a loss of focus?

2. What does "perspective" mean? How does it apply to overcoming temptation?

3. List two common temptations people face today. Discuss where these temptations might lead if we follow through with them. Discuss possible escape routes.

4. Why does it seem natural to blame others for our mistakes? Is it merely human nature? Is our culture to blame? Why is accepting responsibility so difficult, yet so important?

5. Read Matthew 4:1-11. How are the devil's methods of temptation in this passage similar to those he used in Genesis 3?

4

GIVING YOUR BEST
WHEN YOU'VE
BEEN BESTED
Genesis 4

In my eighth-grade gym class, the school year opened and closed with a pentathlon (five-event contest). The purpose of this exercise was to see how each member of the class progressed in physical fitness over the course of the year. Some people performed better at the end of the year than they had at the beginning. A few performed worse. But several in the class – including me – simply did not try hard the second time around. We thought it was "cool" to go lazily through our events. Then graduation day came. All those who performed better in the second pentathlon were recognized and were given an award. I was embarrassed. I had failed to do my best.

> We are to give our best whatever we do. This principle applies to both our secular and our spiritual lives.

I was not the strongest or the fastest or the most athletic. But I knew that I could have performed better. The Bible teaches us that it is wrong not to give our best: "And whatever you do, do it heartily, as to the Lord and not to men, knowing that from the Lord you will receive the reward of the inheritance; for you serve the Lord Christ" (Colossians 3:23-24).

This passage shows that we are to give our best whatever we do. This principle applies to both our secular and our spiritual lives. We work our jobs as though Christ Himself is our boss. This means no more surf sessions on the Internet, no more call-ins to that radio show giving away concert tickets. We don't work for men. As Christians, we work for Christ.

The same is true for service in the church. Bible classes should never be prepared an hour before they are taught. One should never think, "That's the preacher's job." If I identify an act of Christian service that needs to be done, I need to do what I can to make sure it gets done. *Everything* we do, whether in speech or in life, must bring honor to the Lord (Colossians 3:17).

Cain failed on two fronts. First, he failed to offer the best he had. As a result, his worship was not acceptable to God. Second, he failed to do his best when he had been bested. He was the ultimate sore loser. He could have learned from his brother's better offering. Instead, he murdered his brother. We must learn to do our best, even when someone is better than we are.

> **We don't work for men. As Christians, we work for Christ.**

Doing Our Best in Worship

Worship involves two elements: act and attitude. Jesus said this when He told the woman at the well, "God is Spirit, and those who worship Him must worship in spirit and truth" (John 4:24). Our "spirit" refers to our attitude toward worship. Are we focused on the words of the song? Are we listening and following the sermon? "Truth" refers to how the worship is conducted (the act of worship). A rock band leading the song service may be found in many modern churches, but we do not find rock bands in the New Testament. Worship must be conducted in a biblical way.

Cain failed in both his act and his attitude. We read that "Cain brought an offering of the fruit of the ground to the LORD" (Genesis 4:3). Then the Bible says that Abel "brought of the firstborn of his flock and of their fat" (v. 4). The firstborn was considered the most valuable (Exodus 13:2). Also, the fat portions of the animal were considered the best (29:13). They were always to be offered to God (Leviticus 3:9). So Abel offered the best parts of the best animals in his possession. No such remark was made about Cain's offering. He simply brought "an offering." Apparently, he was careless in his worship. He did not offer his best.

Are we careless in our worship? Are we offering our best? Are we more like Cain or more like Abel? A teenage boy was once asked to read Scripture on Sunday morning. He walked to the podium equipped with nothing more than his iPhone. When he had to swipe the screen to continue reading, it became stuck as it tried to load the next page. The application then crashed and would not reload fast enough for him to continue his reading. An awkward silence held this terrified teenager to his place with nothing to do or say. This story exemplifies a lack of preparation. He should have prepared by testing his application and by making sure the scripture loaded properly.

I admit it is difficult to always offer our best in worship. We experience a number of potential distractions. Standing before the congregation, preachers see it all. We are familiar with the gentleman who seems to be on a weekly sleep-timer for the duration of the sermon. We observe the text-and-giggle teenager. But we also note the note-takers. We appreciate those who act as though they hang on to every word when even we know that every word is not a cliffhanger. Every preacher I know has his focus points – people within the congregation who are always listening and offering feedback with their facial expressions. These are the real encouragers because they are engaged in worship.

Are we careless in our worship?
Are we offering our best?
Are we more like Cain or more like Abel?

Perhaps many of you reading this book have never thought about how your behavior in worship affects others. But think about it now. Here are some helpful hints that would have assisted Cain and can perhaps assist all of us as participants in public worship.

Prepare for Worship

This starts before we ever arrive at the building. My father would not allow television on Sunday mornings. He believed that we should be preparing our minds to worship God. He wanted to make sure that Sunday morning was treated differently than the other days of the week in our home. This custom definitely made an impression. It is important for us to be thinking about the worship we will offer to God before we begin to do it.

Do you have a Bible class lesson? Read over it. Read the scriptures that go along with it. Are you scheduled to teach a class or to read a scripture? Study your lesson. Read your passage many times over to get it in your mind. You want to be prepared.

What about how we dress? Is our clothing going to be distracting? Is our perfume or cologne so strong that others won't be able to get a whiff of fresh air? Are our collars wrinkled or our dresses stained? Are we wearing too much gold? These are just a few of the questions that ought to be on our minds before we ever leave our homes. We must remember the purpose of our worship. We are not there to socialize or to broadcast our wealth. Cain forgot the true purpose of worship. Let us not repeat his error.

Focus on Worship

When we arrive at the church building, we should be prepared to worship. But we should also focus on the events of the service. If a Scripture reading is announced, follow along with it. If a prayer is prayed, try to concentrate on every word. When the teacher begins to teach or when the preacher begins to preach, take notes. Preachers and teachers may seem boring at times. They may seem to be talking over our heads. But you will be amazed at how much more you learn when you take notes. You will get *out of* worship what you put *into* worship. Worship isn't all about us, but it is certainly appropriate for us to be encouraged in our worship to God (Hebrews 10:25).

Cain obviously put very little into worship. Abel offered an animal sacrifice. This meant that the animal had to be killed and certain body parts had to be removed; then it had to be carried to the place where it was to be offered to God (see the procedures in Leviticus 1). Cain, on the other hand, essentially offered a salad. Which one required more preparation? Which one required more focus?

Cain did not skip the worship service. He was there and was involved. But just being in the right place was not enough.

Both Cain and Abel made offerings. This is important. Cain did not skip the worship service. He was there and was involved. But just being in the right place was not enough. The *quality* of his worship was poor, so God rejected his worship. It is possible for us to be so distracted by the outside world that we fail to offer acceptable worship.

Distractions are all around us in a worship service. Someone has a funny-sounding sneeze. A baby begins to cry. A family walks in late.

The lady behind you sings too loudly. The man next to her is off-key. … The list is endless. This is why worship requires focus. The next worship service you attend, try thinking about the meaning of every word of every song. Try following the preacher's words and taking notes. Try praying along with the prayer leaders. See if it doesn't make a difference in the quality of your worship.

Reflect on Worship

Has anyone ever asked you on Sunday afternoon what the preacher talked about on Sunday morning? Were you able to answer correctly? It is important that, throughout the week, we think about the sermons, the classes and the lessons we learn. Reflection on the Bible's teaching will strengthen us and help us to grow spiritually.

The worship of the church is just a small part of our week. There are 168 hours in every week, of which we may spend three and a half in worship. If we attended school for only half a day, one day per week, we wouldn't learn very much. In the same way, we can learn only a limited amount from the sermons and classes in our churches. Therefore, it is vital that we continue to study throughout the week. Go over the notes you took on the sermons and Bible classes. Think about the lessons that were offered. Your relationship with God depends largely on knowing and understanding Him. This only begins in the church service.

> **Your relationship with God depends largely on knowing and understanding Him. This only begins in the church service.**

What If Someone Else Is Better?

Worship should never be a competition, but many people try to turn it into one. Who is the best song leader? Who is best at reading Scripture? Is our associate minister a better preacher than our pulpit man? These are questions we should never ask. We are in no position to decide. The audience of our worship is God Himself, not human beings (Hebrews 12:28).

Cain forgot this lesson. He became so jealous of his brother that he "rose up against Abel his brother and killed him" (Genesis 4:8). Cain failed to give his best when someone else was better. Rather than being motivated to do better himself, Cain became angry and killed his brother. When we find that others are better, we should work hard to improve. Sometimes our best is not as good as someone else's. That's okay. We should encourage those who are better. We should ask them for help so that we can improve. Cain's pride was his ultimate sin.

I remember a song service a few years ago where I noticed the man in front of me holding one finger in his right ear. My singing was obviously not on par with his standards! It's good that I wasn't singing for *him*. I was singing as well as I could to my Lord. Many people would become upset or offended to see something like that. They might even stop singing or become very quiet in their singing. Instead, when a situation like that occurs, we should ask ourselves the questions that Paul asked: "For am I now seeking the approval of man, or of God? Or am I trying to please man? If I were still trying to please man, I would not be a servant of Christ" (Galatians 1:10 ESV).

> **We should remember always to do our best, recognizing that we are working for God and not for people.**

We can always do our best even when others are better. God apparently did not want everyone to have a beautiful voice, or He would have made us that way. But He did instruct us all to sing (Ephesians 5:19; Colossians 3:16). We should remember always to do our best, recognizing that we are working for God and not for people (v. 23).

Conclusion

In the 2008 Summer Olympics in Beijing, China, tae kwan do competitor Angel Matos did the unthinkable. After an injury timeout, Matos failed to return to the mat, and the referee disqualified him for violating the rules. After an intense argument with the referee, Matos kicked him in the face, pushed a judge, and spat on the floor before he was eventually led out of the arena. As a result, Matos was banned from the sport for life.

This is an example of someone who failed. He had been bested. Yet he did not give his best. His name is disgraced in his sport forever. We face challenges on a daily basis. We face others who are attempting to "best" us. We can survive these challenges by remembering that our worship and our lives are dedicated to God. If we give our best to God, "We may boldly say: 'The LORD is my helper; I will not fear. What can man do to me?'" (Hebrews 13:6).

Discussion Questions

1. What two elements should be involved in worship according to Jesus (John 4:24)? How are these elements involved?

2. List some things we can do to prepare our minds for worship. How does preparation help us in other parts of life? How can preparation enhance the quality of our worship?

3. List some things we can do to focus our minds during the worship service.

4. Read Colossians 3:23-24 again. How does this apply to our lives?

5

STAYING AFLOAT
IN A
FLOOD OF EVIL
Genesis 6-8

Noah's ark is one of the most familiar stories in the Bible. We often playfully imagine all those animals and speculate about life on the ark. Was it crowded? Did it stink? Were there any dinosaurs? These questions may be interesting to ask, but the story of Noah's ark is not a playful story. In fact, it is one of the saddest stories in human history.

Imagine a different scene than is usually considered. Think of the helpless screams erupting from the waters. Picture the sinners banging on the ark, begging to be pulled aboard. Imagine the parents who watched their crying toddlers drown, and the animals beating their paws and hooves against the water, struggling to avoid death. And after the shrill screaming ended, imagine the eerie silence that fell over the waters. Noah's ark is *not* the fun story of a floating zoo. It is the story of death. It is about sin and the consequences of evil in the world.

The Flood of Evil

Before the earth was flooded with water, it had been flooded with evil. The Bible reports that "the wickedness of man was great in the earth, and that every intent of the thoughts of his heart was only evil continually" (Genesis 6:5). Noah lived in a time when wickedness was rampant. Sadly, wickedness thrives even today. Many are falling into the same temptation traps we find recorded of the generation of the flood. Notice the following descriptions.

Sight and Sin Are Connected

What they *saw* led them to sin. The Bible says, "The sons of God saw the daughters of men, that they were beautiful; and they took wives for themselves of all whom they chose" (Genesis 6:2). The righteous people ("sons of God") *saw* the unrighteous ("daughters of men"). As a result, they were enticed to sin. There is no indication that the sons of God *thought* about the consequences of their actions. They simply responded to their animal lusts and selfishly "took ... for themselves." Their sight led them to sin.

> **Our prayer should be the same as David's: "I will set nothing wicked before my eyes; I hate the work of those who fall away; it shall not cling to me" (Psalm 101:3).**

One example of the danger of sight today is what we view on the Internet. The Internet is a helpful tool and can be used with great benefit. However, our smartphones, tablets and computers can also present to us a flood of evil. It can be difficult to stay afloat. A 2008 study revealed that 93 percent of boys and 62 percent of girls were exposed to Internet pornography before the age of 18.[1] Our eyes can lead us to see things that are unholy. Our prayer should be the same as David's: "I will set nothing wicked before my eyes; I hate the work of those who fall away; it shall not cling to me" (Psalm 101:3).

Selfishness and Sin Are Connected

Not only were the "sons of God" enticed to sin by what they saw but also by their selfishness. Listen to the Bible again: "The sons of God saw the daughters of men, that they were beautiful; and they took wives for themselves of all whom they chose" (Genesis 6:2). The term "beautiful" in the Hebrew language (in which Genesis was written originally) is literally "good" (*tov*). It is the same word used to describe Eve's evaluation of the fruit on the forbidden tree: "the woman saw that the tree was *good* for food" (3:6, emphasis added).

The term "good" implies an evaluation of worth. Some people like coconut. I cannot stand it. Some people like onions. I do not. My evaluation of what is good is different from that of others. We can differ on our opinions of what is good, but what God calls good, we cannot call evil. Because the sons of God saw what *they* considered good, they "took ... for themselves of all whom *they chose*" (emphasis added). They never considered how their decision might have affected their spirituality.

How to Stay Afloat

Perhaps no servant of God was under more pressure than Noah. Although everyone was wicked, Noah managed to do good. The Bible says of him: "Noah was a just man, perfect in his generations. Noah walked with God" (Genesis 6:9). How did Noah maintain his faithfulness? How was Noah able to stay afloat? Consider the following characteristics of Noah.

Noah Took a Stand

Peter recorded that Noah was "a preacher of righteousness" (2 Peter 2:5). When everyone else was doing evil, Noah was preaching what was good. Christians are often silent about their faith. They are afraid to share righteousness with friends. What if we are rejected? What if we say the wrong thing? The what-ifs could go on and on, but we can summarize with this basic principle: We are afraid to fail.

> If we wish to be righteous in our generations, we must expect rejection.

But think about Noah. If preachers are measured in terms of results, Noah failed miserably. In fact, Noah may have been one of the least successful preachers ever. Noah had 120 years to preach his message of righteousness (Genesis 6:3). He also had a huge boat to serve as a perfect object lesson, illustrating God's future destruction. Yet he converted only seven people – all members of his own family. If Noah were a modern missionary, his support would be withdrawn! It goes without saying that Noah was repeatedly rejected. If we wish to be righteous in our generations, we must expect rejection as well.

Noah Obeyed God

Noah was willing to do whatever God asked him to do – no matter what the cost. Consider the following: (1) Noah was asked to accept the concept of a global flood when he had never seen rain (Genesis 2:5);

(2) Noah was asked to believe that all mankind would be destroyed (6:13, 17); (3) Noah was commanded to build a boat under very strict orders, despite an apparent lack of expertise in doing so (vv. 15-16); (4) Noah was commanded to corral a multiplicity of creatures, some naturally ferocious. Although some people believe that a miracle must have been involved here, the Bible never mentions it (vv. 19-21). To all of these requests, the Bible simply summarizes: "Thus Noah did; according to all that God commanded him, so he did" (v. 22). Oh, that we would all be so submissive!

We can only imagine the criticisms Noah must have heard from his peers. No one outside of his family believed in what he was do-ing. Perhaps Noah felt much the way Elijah did when he was persecuted by Jezebel's henchmen: "The children of Israel have forsaken Your covenant, torn down Your altars, and killed Your prophets with the sword. I alone am left" (1 Kings 19:10). Imagine how alone Noah must have felt. It is easier to remain faithful when everyone is faithful. True obedience is measured by how we react when we are forced to stand alone.

> **True obedience is measured by how we react when we are forced to stand alone.**

Conclusion

The story of Noah is about much more than a floating zoo in a flood. It is about sin and its consequences. God is loving and gracious and kind, but He is also fair (Exodus 34:6-7). It would be unfair of God to treat sinners the same way He treats the righteous. The story of the flood proves this lesson.

God was heartbroken when He saw the evil in the world. The Bible records, "And the LORD was sorry that He had made man on the earth, and He was grieved in His heart" (Genesis 6:6). God's grief motivated Him to destroy the world. He was grieved precisely because He is fair. He had no other option than to destroy the world He had created.

Noah was saved from the destruction because he stood up for righteousness when no one else would. As a result, he and his fam-ily were rescued from death. Peter wrote about the spirits in prison, who formerly were disobedient, when once the Divine longsuffering waited in the days of Noah, while the ark was being prepared, in which a few, that is, eight souls, were saved through water. There is also an antitype which now saves us – baptism (not the removal of the filth of the flesh, but the answer of a good conscience toward God), through the resurrection of Jesus Christ. (1 Peter 3:20-21)

Just as the ark was able to save the eight people in it, baptism is now capable of saving all those who submit to it.

God needs volunteers for righteousness now as much as ever. We live in a world in which wickedness abounds and righteousness is mocked. Preachers and congregations may fall into worldliness, "teaching as doctrines the commandments of men" (Matthew 15:9), but God's standard of living will always have a place in our world. Righteousness is needed most when it seems most absent.

We live in a world in which wickedness abounds and righteousness is mocked.

Discussion Questions

1. Name some ways in which the typical view of the flood story differs from what is presented in the Bible.

2. List three positive qualities of standing out for your faith. Name biblical characters other than Noah who were rewarded for standing out for their faith.

3. Name at least two lessons we can learn from the "sons of God" when they fell victim to temptation. Why did they fall away from God?

4. Name at least two ways Noah demonstrated his righteousness, explaining why he was declared faithful and blameless.

6

DANGERS
OF
DRUNKENNESS
Genesis 9

The sin of drunkenness is one of the most challenging pressures facing society today. The pressure is strong because American culture accepts and endorses alcohol consumption. To a degree, we even endorse public intoxication. In 2013, a video clip of a pathetic drunk attempting to walk up a hill went viral. The popularity of such a video leaves the impression that drunkenness is funny. Is foolish behavior ever funny?

Was it funny, in 2013, when an intoxicated Buffalo Bills fan fell on top of an innocent man from the upper deck of Ralph Wilson Stadium? Was it funny when, earlier in the same season, a New York Jets fan punched a woman in a drunken brawl? These senseless acts are not taking place in fraternity houses and sports bars. They are happening in alleged family-friendly environments – all due to the abuse of alcohol.

The problem is not limited to sporting events, though, and the problem, sadly, does not begin with adults. Although laws exist in every state governing the age of those allowed to consume alcoholic beverages, almost everyone will acknowledge that these laws do not prevent young people from experimenting with alcohol. By the time some of them reach legal drinking age, they are already dependent upon it. Not only is alcohol abuse forbidden in the Scriptures, modern human experience teaches us the dangers of alcohol.

A Look at the Facts

Excessive alcohol consumption leads to approximately 88,000 deaths each year in the U.S.[1] By contrast, cocaine kills only about 10,000

Not only is alcohol abuse forbidden in the Scriptures, modern human experience teaches us the dangers of alcohol.

people in the U.S. each year.[2] Yet no advertising campaigns with tanned bikini models and handsome hunks promote crack, and there is no drug task force crack down on beer. If any other drug killed 88,000 people each year, it would be made illegal as soon as lawmakers could put the paperwork together. But not alcohol.

Alcohol factors into approximately 31 percent of traffic-related deaths each year.[3] In fact, excessive alcohol use is the third-leading lifestyle-related cause of death in the U.S.[4] And according to the National Council on Alcoholism and Drug Dependence, alcohol is a factor in 40 percent of all violent crimes today, including 37 percent of rapes and sexual assaults.[5] The statistics may differ from study to study, but one fact is undeniable: Alcohol is dangerous. Yet Americans continue to use and abuse alcohol.

According to the National Institute of Alcohol Abuse and Alcoholism, more than 50 percent of teens have taken at least one drink by age 15. By age 18, more than 70 percent of teens have had at least one drink. It is staggering to note that young people between the ages of 12 and 20 years old account for 11 percent of the alcohol consumed in the U.S. each year.[6] The alcohol culture in our country is growing worse and worse, and the collateral damage is only growing more apparent.

As people who are to be holy as God is holy (Leviticus 19:2), Christians must pay attention to the dangers of alcohol. Regardless of what others are doing, we must recognize the immense temptation and avoid this evil in our lives. Furthermore, we must continue to encourage our children and young people to stay away from the dangers of drunkenness.

Noah's Drunkenness

Noah was the first man in history to plant a vineyard and to drink alcoholic wine. The Bible says of him: "And Noah began to be a farmer, and he planted a vineyard. Then he drank of the wine and was drunk, and became uncovered in his tent" (Genesis 9:20-21). This passage does not censure Noah for his drinking. Likely, Noah was unaware of the dangers of alcoholic wine. He did not have access to statistics, knowledge of alcohol-related deaths, or rehabilitation facilities for substance abuse. Nevertheless, we must acknowledge that the mysterious events that follow in Genesis 9 would have been avoided if Noah had not become drunk. Drunkenness led to Noah making bad decisions. These bad decisions affected the future of his family (vv. 25-27).

I know a young man who climbed into a car with a drunk driver. After a horrific accident and months of rehabilitation, he survived, but he is now paralyzed. He will never walk again. His story, unfortunately, is not unusual. Although he was more fortunate than some, that decision will affect the rest of his life.

Noah likely had no idea what would happen as a result of his taking just one drink. Just one drink of whiskey may not seem to be such a bad thing. We may rationalize: "After all, cough syrup has alcohol in it. One shot of whiskey is no different than a shot of cold medicine." Most of us have consumed alcohol in small quantities

> **There is a difference between taking medicine and getting drunk.**

without even knowing it. But there is a difference between taking medicine and getting drunk (cf. 1 Timothy 5:23).

Alcohol and Biblical Culture

Nowhere does the Bible forbid drinking alcoholic beverages in small quantities (if it did, it would be sinful to take a spoonful of cough syrup). But the Bible consistently condemns drunkenness as a sin. The authors of Scripture recognize that alcohol is very dangerous and must be treated with respect. But if alcohol consumption is potentially dangerous, why doesn't the Bible just rule against it entirely?

We should keep three factors in mind about wine in the biblical world: (1) All fruit beverages have the potential to become alcoholic; (2) fermentation in biblical times generally occurred by natural means rather than by chemical processes (as today); and (3) wine in biblical times was usually mixed with another liquid, typically water.

First, in the biblical world, there were no refrigerators. As a result, the natural sugars in grapes or other fruits slowly broke down and eventually made their drinks alcoholic. Because the water in many places was unsafe to drink and because milk would have spoiled within a few hours, fruit beverages were the only practical option for drinking. "New wine" or "sweet wine" was favorable, but wine made in large quantities would not remain sweet for long. Within a day or two, the wine would become slightly alcoholic.

Catalysts are injected into modern alcoholic beverages to make them much more alcoholic.

Within weeks or months, it would become more so. After the harvest, wine would be made and stored, usually in cool places (buried partially underground or, where possible, stored in caves). Generally, the people attempted to slow the fermentation process, but they could never stop it entirely.

Second, although the ancient world attests to drinking alcoholic beverages, we should mention that, in general, these beverages were allowed to ferment naturally. Catalysts are injected into modern alcoholic beverages to make them much more alcoholic much more quickly than nature would allow. In the biblical world, most people would have neither the ability nor the interest to increase the alcoholic content of their beverages. Of course, there have always been "drunks"; hence, there has always been a market for highly alcoholic beverages (Proverbs 23:29-30; Joel 3:3).

Third, alcoholic beverages were normally mixed with water to dilute the alcohol and to purify the water. In the Greek and Roman worlds, many ratios were recommended: 20 parts water to one part wine,[7] eight parts water to one part wine,[8] and so on. In later times, it seems that the three-to-one ratio was generally accepted. To put this into perspective, a 12-ounce glass would contain only three ounces of wine and nine ounces of water. When we keep in mind that biblical wine generally had a much lower alcohol content than wine today, it becomes very clear that biblical wine-drinking really cannot be compared to wine-drinking today. As one author remarks,

> To consume the amount of alcohol that is in two martinis
> by drinking wine containing three parts water to one part

wine, one would have to drink over twenty-two glasses. In other words, it is possible to become intoxicated from wine mixed with three parts of water, but one's drinking would probably affect the bladder long before it affected the mind.[9]

This assessment does not even take into account the much higher alcohol content of a modern martini in comparison with biblical wines.

A Higher Standard

Despite the common practice of drinking wine in biblical times, the Bible makes clear that God's ideal situation is that wine be avoided altogether. The priests were God's chosen representatives to His people. Therefore, they were asked to live by a higher standard than other Israelites. When they were worshiping God publicly, the Bible states: "Do not drink wine or intoxicating drink, you, nor your sons with you, when you go into the tabernacle of meeting, lest you die. It shall be a statute forever throughout your generations" (Leviticus 10:9). If the priests drank any wine at all, they would be struck dead.

Nazirites were people who had taken a vow for a limited period of time. They were to avoid contact with the dead, cutting their hair, and all contact with wine or any product of the vine (Numbers 6:2-8). Although they could drink wine at the end of their vow (v. 20), it was clear that a higher standard was imposed upon them for the period of their dedication to God.

> Despite the common practice of drinking wine in biblical times, the Bible makes clear that God's ideal situation is that wine be avoided altogether.

King Lemuel, in the book of Proverbs, added that kings are to avoid wine. He stated: "It is not for kings, O Lemuel, it is not for kings to drink wine, nor for princes intoxicating drink; lest they drink and forget the law, and pervert the justice of all the afflicted" (31:4-5). Here it is clear that a king must maintain a clear focus, and alcohol would lead him to bad decisions. A king must administer the justice of God. With alcohol in his system, he fails to represent God's standard of living.

Conclusion

Despite all the warnings available today, alcohol continues to be a problem in our world. The church can serve as a center for the prevention of alcoholism. We can help those who fall into the trap of alcoholism. But to do so we must warn about the dangers of alcohol. We must emphasize the ruin it brings to families and to lives. Consider the effect Noah's drunkenness had on his family. Although Shem and Japheth covered Noah without looking, Ham was cursed to serve his brothers (Genesis 9:18-27). We must highlight the bad judgment that typically follows the consumption of alcohol. Solomon taught this very thing in Proverbs 23:29-35:

> Who has woe? Who has sorrow? Who has contentions? Who has complaints? Who has wounds without cause? Who has redness of eyes? Those who linger long at the wine, those who go in search of mixed wine. Do not look on the wine when it is red, when it sparkles in the cup, when it swirls around smoothly; at the last it bites like a serpent, and stings like a viper. Your eyes will see strange things, and your heart will utter perverse things. Yes, you will be like one who lies down in the midst of the sea or like one who lies at the top of the mast, saying: "They have struck me, but I was not hurt; they have beaten me, but I did not feel it. When shall I awake, that I may seek another drink?"

Discussion Questions

1. Why do you think drinking alcohol is so popular when it is so dangerous?

2. List three cultural differences between wine-drinking in the biblical world and wine-drinking today. How should these differences affect how Christians view alcohol today?

3. Imagine your son or daughter, grandson or granddaughter, is arrested for public intoxication. How would you communicate the dangers of alcohol to him or her?

7

BABBLE IN BABEL

Genesis 11

The Bible's Babel story can be listed among the childhood favorites. Every child is excited when imagining a massive tower reaching high into the clouds. Even as adults we can appreciate the time, expense and engineering that would have gone into such a building project (see Luke 14:28-30). But a powerful message of warning is behind the narrative. The Tower of Babel account is not a fairy tale, nor is it a monument to human ingenuity and structural engineering. Rather, the Tower of Babel is a memorial to disobedience.

A Story of "Firsts"

The disobedience of the Babel builders led to a number of "firsts" in human history. For instance, at Babel, for the first time in history, human language was confused. Both the Bible and other writings from the Old Testament world attest to a common language among all humans. A tablet dating to about the time of Abraham says, "The whole universe, the people in unison, to Enlil [a Mesopotamian god] in one tongue gave praise."[1] This Mesopotamian myth projects an early time in human history when everyone spoke the same language. Like the Bible, other ancient peoples recognized the original unity of human language.

Another "first" that the Tower of Babel story reveals is the first attempt to build a city. Nothing is wrong with building cities. Elsewhere in the Old Testament, God even commanded the Israelites to build cities (Numbers 32:24). What made the building of Babel sinful was the timing of its construction. Sometimes people can do the right thing at the wrong time. Nothing is wrong with gathering sticks, but the man who did so on the Sabbath was killed for his sin (Numbers 15:32-36).

Sometimes people can do the right thing at the wrong time.

Nothing is wrong with playing golf or fishing, but doing these things on a Sunday morning rather than attending worship is displeasing to God. God had commanded mankind to "be fruitful and multiply" and "fill the earth" (Genesis 1:28; 9:1). Settling in one location (a city) prevented the people of Babel from following the command to fill the earth. As a result, God made a point of scattering the people to prevent their disobedience.

Third, the Babel story tells about the first attempt to construct a skyscraper. Noah's ark was a large boat (450 feet long, 75 feet wide, and 45 feet high), but it would have been dwarfed by the massive Tower of Babel. Sometimes people think that the tower builders were trying to reach God because the Bible says the tower's top was in the heavens. Whether the builders actually believed they could do so, we cannot know. The text does make a point of saying that "the LORD came *down* to see the city and the tower" (Genesis 11:5, emphasis added). If the builders were trying to reach God, they were not even close. But there may be another element to the story.

People in ancient times believed that a higher elevation put them closer to their gods. About the Babylonian king Hammurabi, who lived some 400 years before Moses, it is boasted, "He made the image of the goddess Inanna of Kibalbarru 'as high as the sky.'"[2] This quotation leads us to wonder whether the Tower of Babel was a monument to God (or a god) for worship. Archaeologists have discovered a number of large structures from Mesopotamia known as ziggurats. These were artificial mountains with rows of stairs built into them. The purpose of a ziggurat was twofold. First, one could climb to the top in order to be "closer" to the gods. Second, a temple was constructed at the top of the structure to invite the gods to enter. If the Tower of Babel was not a cylindrical tower (as we often imagine) but a structure similar to a ziggurat, then it may have been constructed as an object for worship – an object that the Lord had not commanded. This might be yet another "first."

Motivations for Building

The city of Babel and its tower were visible for miles. Without a doubt, they attracted the attention of people throughout the region of southern Mesopotamia. But their reasons for building were sinful. The text reveals that the people were motivated (1) to make a name for themselves and (2) to avoid dispersion throughout the earth. As a result, they were punished.

Making a Name for Myself: The Sin of Selfishness

A good name is a good thing. Solomon declared, "A good name is to be chosen rather than great riches, loving favor rather than silver and gold" (Proverbs 22:1). Again he wrote, "A good name is better than precious ointment" (Ecclesiastes 7:1). By the word "name," the Bible simply refers to one's reputation. All of us have reputations. Some are known for being kind; others are known for being mean. I had a friend in junior high school with a reputation for fighting. Very few people wanted to test him because they did not want to get clobbered. Maybe the worst kind of reputation a person can have is one of selfishness.

There are many tell-tale signs of the self-centered person. First, he (or she) lives to be served rather than to serve. He cannot consider how to help other people; he must always be the center of attention. Selfish people suffer from the "I" disease. The parable of the rich man illustrates this problem (Luke 12:16-21); more than 10 times in just three verses (vv. 17-19), the first-person singular pronoun ("I," "my" or "me") is used. The rich man revealed the focal point of his life: himself. Jesus challenged us to be last in order to be first, to serve in order to lead: "For even the Son of Man did not come to be served, but to serve, and to give His life a ransom for many" (Mark 10:45).

One of the worst reputations a person can have is one of selfishness.

Second, selfish people are seldom godly people. This is because self-centered people believe their rules are the most important ones (Romans 2:8). They don't learn to obey God because they have trouble learning how to submit, and they haven't learned to consider others to be more important than themselves (Philippians 2:3). Whether we submit to our spouses, to our bosses, to our teachers, or to our elders, all of us must recognize that we cannot know everything. We cannot *always* get what we want – nor should we. Allowing others the opportunity to benefit should be a great joy in our lives.

The builders of Babel had been given a commandment: "fill the earth" (Genesis 1:28; 9:1). What an opportunity they had! Many of them were brilliant architects and engineers. They learned how to build large cities and towers that were thick and strong. Their gifts would have been beneficial to the entire human race. If they had spread throughout the world, as God had commanded, they would have brought safety and beauty to all people. But rather than allowing their skills to bless the lives of others, the builders of Babel chose to serve themselves (11:4). They became selfish and ungodly, and they suffered for it.

> **Allowing others the opportunity to benefit should be a great joy in our lives.**

"Lest We Be Scattered:" Breaking up Cliques

Everybody is aware of cliques. By the first or second grade, children have perfected the art of forming them. Small groups of people with similar interests band together and exclude all who do not belong in their group. Schools, businesses and even churches can develop dangerous cliques. The citizens of Babel were, in some ways, one big clique. They built a city for themselves and kept everyone else out.

Cliques keep us from branching out. They eliminate the possibility of making new – even "different" – friends. They keep us from learning about people outside of our group. During my college days, I remember seeing another student eating by himself. He looked lonely, and he was certainly different. I remember feeling sorry for him. At the same time, the people in my clique didn't really know him. So I sat with my friends and watched the lonely student eat all by himself. Whether he wanted to be by himself or not, I should have taken the opportunity to get to know him better.

As Christians, we need to be a friend to those without friends. We need to reach out to those who are "different" or who do not have the clothing we wear or the wealth we amass. We need to stand up for justice, love and kindness. Cliques have lasted long enough, especially in the church. Let's recognize the talents of other people. Let's strive to involve everyone in the work of the Lord.

Every human being has unique talents that can benefit both himself and others. Some are deeply compassionate and can offer advice to those in need. Others can teach or preach publicly. Others can help decorate a classroom. Whatever talents we may have, we should and must use them to

> **Cliques have lasted long enough, especially in the church. Let's recognize the talent of other people. Let's strive to involve everyone in the work of the Lord.**

serve the Lord. We must help others realize their potential as well. The builders of Babel wished to serve the citizens of their city rather than to serve mankind. Their selfishness became the reason for their loss. They did not like how other people lived, so they created a city and excluded everyone else. But their behavior displeased the Lord.

Conclusion

Although abandoned after God confused the people's language, the city of Babel was eventually reinhabited and rebuilt, and it was a constant problem for God's people in the Old Testament. The city eventually became an empire that oppressed and exiled Judah in the early sixth century B.C. The name of the city was Babylon ("Babel" and "Babylon" are the same word in Hebrew). Although the city of Babylon no longer exists, the sinful behavior of its first builders does. People continue to be selfish. People continue to build cities around themselves and their small cliques. Let us remember that we serve a God who loves the entire world (John 3:16). Should we do any less?

Discussion Questions

1. Discuss the three "firsts" of Genesis 11.

2. What were the two purposes of building the Tower of Babel?

3. Identify some of the unique talents people in your congregation have. How can they use those talents to help other people? What can you do to encourage others to use their talents for the Lord?

4. Discuss what a life of service might look like. What kinds of things do service-oriented people do?

8

ABRAHAM:
SERVICE AND
SACRIFICE
Genesis 12-24

Abraham is a celebrity in the religious world. To the Jews, he is the father of Isaac and the ancestor of their race. To the Christians, he is a spiritual father, the forerunner to those seeking to be justified by faith in God (Romans 4:11). To the Muslims, he is the father of Ishmael, the forefather of the Arabian peoples. Abraham's fame might lead us to exaggerate his accomplishments and his faithfulness to God, for Abraham was also a man who struggled in service.

Like all of us, Abraham made mistakes. He had moments of remarkable faith, and he had moments of complete failure. Yet throughout his life, despite his mistakes, he was faithful to God. The Bible sums up his life: "Abraham believed God, and it was accounted to him for righteousness" (Romans 4:3; Galatians 3:6; James 2:23; cf. Genesis 15:6). The New Testament book of Hebrews gives a full 12 verses to the faithful life of Abraham (11:8-19) – twice the material given to any other character. This great chapter shows that we do not have to allow our mistakes to define us. We can, like Abraham, recover from sin and live faithful lives before God.

> Like Abraham, we can recover from sin and live faithful lives before God.

From Abram to Abraham
We first meet Abraham as Abram. The name means "exalted father."

Why God chose Abram to be special is unclear, but the choice proves to be a good one as Abram grows in his faith to become Abraham, meaning "father of a multitude." Still, his faith had to develop. Even though the "exalted father" (Abram) was chosen by God, he was yet to be "justified" by his faith. Only after establishing a track record of faithful obedience is the initial promise realized and symbolized in his name Abraham ("father of multitudes," Genesis 17:5).

First, Abram had to overcome his family's religious weakness. Abram came from a family of idol-worshipers (Joshua 24:2). In fact, the family moved away from Ur of the Chaldeans to a city called Haran (Genesis 11:31). Haran was well-known as a place for the worship of the moon god Sin (having nothing to do with the English word "sin"). Although Abram's parents may or may not have moved to Haran to worship this false god, it seems unlikely that they taught him about the true God. Maybe they did not know the truth themselves. In any case, Abram had to overcome a bad family situation.

Second, Abram had to overcome the fear of the unknown. God did not tell Abram where to go (Genesis 12:1). He just told him to leave his family and homeland. At this time, sons were expected to remain with their families. Society was based on family connections. Obviously, the larger the family, the wealthier and more influential they could become. For Abram, leaving his family meant that he would never see them again.

He accepted the promise by faith, yet his faith would be challenged throughout his life.

Third, Abram had to overcome uncertainty. Sarai was 65 years old and had no children. At this time, sons were the pride of the family. A woman who could not have children – especially sons – was viewed as having lesser value. Some ancient marriage contracts even allowed the man to marry another wife if the first wife could not have children.[1] God promised to Abram a great nation (Genesis 12:2). Obviously a nation must have an ancestor, so the promise implied at least one child. But Abram had no guarantee. He simply accepted the promise by faith (Hebrews 11:8), yet his faith would be challenged throughout his life.

Challenges to Faith

As Christians, we face constant challenges to our faith. Abraham too faced at least four specific challenges to his faith: (1) the challenge of patience; (2) the challenge of disappointment; (3) the challenge of submission; and (4) the challenge of silence.

The Challenge of Patience

Patience is a difficult yet important virtue to develop. A child waiting for Christmas must learn patience. An applicant waiting to hear about a new job must exercise patience. Patience is necessary for all of us. Patience is a characteristic of love (1 Corinthians 13:4) and a key to healthy relationships (Ephesians 4:2). Patience even assists us in helping those who are spiritually weak (1 Thessalonians 5:14).

Imagine how Abraham must have felt. God promised to make him a great nation (Genesis 12:2), yet he was forced to wait 25 years before the promise was fulfilled. Did Abraham doubt God? Did Abraham ever

> **Patience is a difficult yet important virtue to develop.**

consider going back home? The Bible does not say. But the Bible does teach that he and Sarah took matters into their own hands (16:1-3). They interfered with the plan of God because they were impatient – they had been waiting for 10 years! Perhaps they would have benefited from the promise of Isaiah: "For they shall not be ashamed who wait for Me" (Isaiah 49:23).

The Challenge of Disappointment

Have you ever been crushed with disappointment? As a child, I had convinced myself that I was getting a new four-wheeler for Christmas (a Honda 300EX, which is no longer in production). I received very little for Christmas that year, so naturally I knew something big was coming. My parents told me to close my eyes as the door was opened. When I opened my eyes, I saw my *old* four-wheeler (a Yamaha 80 – far smaller and slower than the 300EX). Rather than buying me a new four-wheeler, my parents had repaired my old one. What a disappointment!

Abraham probably began his journey with a great deal of excitement – the God of the universe had promised him success! In fact, the first promise God made was that He would lead Abraham "to a land" (Genesis 12:1). Abraham traveled more than 400 miles to reach the land of Canaan only to find that there was a famine in the land (v. 10). Abraham had been promised that this unproductive land would belong to his descendants (v. 7) – what a disappointment!

> **Even when gifts do not meet our expectations, we should give "thanks always for all things to God" (Ephesians 5:20).**

Sometimes we are disappointed because our expectations are too high. I should have been thankful that I had a four-wheeler at all. Most youngsters are not so blessed. Abraham should have been grateful that he had received a land that he had not previously owned. Christians must always abound in thanksgiving (Colossians 2:7). Even when gifts do not meet our expectations, we should give "thanks always for all things to God" (Ephesians 5:20). We should be content with what we have (Hebrews 13:5).

The Challenge of Submission

Submission is rarely easy, especially when you don't understand *why* you are being told to do something. Every back-talking child who has ever heard a parent spout off the phrase "because I said so!" can testify to this point. We are not satisfied simply to do; we always want an explanation. However, God expects His servants to submit without asking why. Circumcision of the flesh may seem foolish to us. How could fleshly mutilation secure spiritual faithfulness? Yet Moses was nearly killed because he failed to obey the command (Exodus 4:24-26). Why did it matter if the ark of the covenant was touched? I don't know, but Uzzah lost his life for touching it (2 Samuel 6:6-7).

Imagine Abraham. He had finally received his precious son. He loved Isaac, and he tried to teach him to follow God. But then God commanded Abraham to sacrifice his son (Genesis 22:2). There is no indication that Abraham hesitated or that he tried to bargain with God as he had done earlier (18:23-32). He simply obeyed. In humble submission, he surrendered his will to the will of God.

As readers of the Bible, we might reach the conclusion that Abraham obeyed God only to receive a son. Until we get to Genesis 21, the promise of a son was dangled in front of Abraham and Sarah like a carrot before a horse. But in Genesis 22, we learn that Abraham put God first (cf. Matthew 6:33).

Abraham obeyed God even when God asked him to do something he could not understand. He did not ask why. He simply went. Abraham did not decide on the day of the commandment to submit to God. He had already submitted long before. Obedience is the natural consequence of submission.

The Challenge of Silence

One of the greatest challenges to faith is to decide what to do when you don't know what to do. In other words, how do we choose to obey God when God is silent? What do we do when God has not revealed in the Bible a clear line to follow? Where should you send your children or grandchildren to college? Should you take this new job and move your family? Should you retire now or try to work a few more years? These can be challenging questions, and the answers can affect our spiritual condition a great deal. But God is silent. There is no biblical answer. Whatever course we choose, we just have to "make it work."

What was Abraham to do when God did not tell him what to do?

Abraham had to "make it work" throughout his life. The only way Abraham received the will of God was through direct communication. About 100 years of Abraham's life was recorded in the Bible. He was introduced at 75 and died at 175 (Genesis 12–25). Yet almost all of the biblical material concentrates on a segment of 25 years (Genesis 12–24). Over this extensive period of Abraham's life, God communicated with him a total of only eight times! Abraham certainly faced the challenge of silence. What was Abraham to do when God did not tell him what to do? He had to "make it work." Whatever we choose to do in life, we must do it "in the name of the Lord" (Colossians 3:17).

Conclusion

Abraham's life was filled with challenges. Sometimes he made mistakes. But he became the father of the faithful because of his life of submission. You and I are the spiritual heirs of Abraham. We too can live faithfully and be justified through our obedience to God. Through Christ alone, our salvation comes, and through Him, righteousness is possible (Romans 3:22; 2 Timothy 2:10). The example of Abraham encourages us to keep trying. Even when we sin and make mistakes, we can try again, and by the grace of God, we too can become the righteous of God (Romans 4:3).

Discussion Questions

1. Like Abraham, we must overcome challenges to be faithful to God. List a challenge to faith not mentioned in this lesson and how we might overcome it.

2. What does "patience" mean? How can patience be a challenge for Christians?

3. Describe how your disappointment with another person affected your trust in that person. How might disappointment affect one's relationship with God? How should we handle disappointment?

4. How does the secular world view submission? How can submission to God affect our relationship with others? How does submission relate to faith?

9

NO LAUGHING MATTER:
THE LIFE OF ISAAC
Genesis 17-26

I have heard some strange names. Celebrities especially tend to give their children bizarre names. (Ever heard of baby North West or Pilot Inspektor?) But none of us would think the name Isaac sounds strange. In 2013, 10,005 baby boys in the U.S. were named "Isaac" and so were 7 girls.[1] Yet in the world of Genesis, the name was uncommon. No one else in the Old Testament bore the name Isaac, and it's easy to understand why. The name means "he laughs."

Isaac received his strange name because both his father and his mother laughed when God announced his birth (Genesis 17:17; 18:12-15). Isaac was special. He was the only child of elderly parents. He was the result of God's miraculous work in the natural world. He was the heir of Abraham's fortune and of God's promise to the world. The Bible emphasizes the exceptional nature of Isaac's life as God used him to bless the family of Abraham.

The Exceptional Life of Isaac

Just like his father Abraham, Isaac lived a remarkable life. Because God had promised that Isaac would be the son through whom "all the nations of the earth shall be blessed" (Genesis 22:18; 26:4), Isaac had to survive, take a wife, and have children of his own. These things normally happen over the course of one's life. But as the first child of promise, Isaac's life proved exceptional in a number of ways.

Isaac's "Firsts"

The life of Isaac marked a number of "firsts" in the Bible,[2] the first of which was his miraculous birth. Normally, a man who is 100 years old is incapable of reproduction. The same is true for a woman who is 90. But God was working in the lives of Abraham and Sarah to make their reproduction possible. The second "first" was Isaac's circumcision. God required every 8-day-old male in Abraham's family to be circumcised. This was to symbolize the unique relationship God had with Abraham's family (Genesis 17:10-14). As far as we know from the Bible, Isaac was the first 8-day-old child to be circumcised (21:4). The third "first" was that Isaac marked the first generation to inherit the promise of God. Was God faithful only to Abraham? Would He really continue the promise through Isaac? God answered these questions when He assured Isaac of the promise given to Abraham (26:2-5). Because of this promise, God became the God of Abraham and Isaac (28:13).

> As the first child of promise, Isaac's life proved exceptional in a number of ways.

Isaac's Exceptional Qualities

Isaac was responsible for a remarkable number of exceptional experiences among his faithful family. First, of the three Hebrew Patriarchs, only Isaac kept one wife for life. Abraham took Hagar (Genesis 16:1-3), and later, after the death of Sarah, he took Keturah (25:1). Jacob, Isaac's son, took four wives (29:16-30; 30:4, 9). Yet Isaac spent his entire life with Rebekah, the wife of his youth (cf. Proverbs 5:18). Although Rebekah, like Sarah, would be barren at first, Isaac did not marry a Hagar as his father had done. Second, Isaac spent his entire life in the Promised Land. God promised to give the land of Canaan to Abraham's family (Genesis 12:7), but when a famine arose, Abraham fled to Egypt without God's command (v. 10). Jacob too fled to Padan Aram to avoid Esau's wrath (28:1-5) and, in old age, traveled to Egypt, where he died (46:3; 49:33). Only Isaac stayed in the land of God's promise throughout his life. Third, Isaac lived longer than both Abraham and Jacob. Abraham was 175 years old at his death (25:7), and Jacob was 147 years old when he died (47:28). But Isaac died at the age of 180 (35:28)! No one born after the flood lived longer than Isaac.

The Righteous Life of Isaac

We can learn from the Bible that God was directing much of the action in Isaac's life. But Isaac proved himself worthy of the promise through his own decisions. Like Abraham, Isaac was faithful to God and demonstrated his right to the promise by humble obedience.

Family Failure

Isaac remained righteous in the face of family problems. He faced the challenge of two mothers. His mother, Sarah, and his step-mother, Hagar, did not get along (Genesis 16:6; 21:10). Isaac had every reason to join his mother in opposition to his step-brother and step-mother. First, Isaac was the child of promise. Ishmael was never intended to be the child of promise (17:18-19). The special status of favored children is usually recognized from an early time in their lives. Isaac must have known that his mother loved him far more than she loved his step-brother, Ishmael. Second, Sarah was Abraham's first and most important wife. There is no indication that Hagar was as important in the family as her mistress. Sarah's insistence was the only reason Hagar was allowed to become Abraham's wife in the first place (16:2). As a mere servant, Hagar (and so Ishmael) had a lower status in the family. So Isaac must have been a spoiled brat, right? Wrong.

Isaac was faithful to God and demonstrated his right to the promise by humble obedience.

Many people today can identify with the feelings Hagar and Ishmael must have felt. They were second-class citizens in their own family. Yet there is no indication that Isaac treated them the way Sarah did. Isaac was just a baby when Ishmael was driven away from home (Genesis 21:10-14). However, Abraham apparently remained close to Hagar and Ishmael (in the region of Beersheba) for the rest of his life (vv. 14, 22-34; 22:19), and it seems that Isaac had some kind of a relationship with Ishmael because the two men buried their father together (25:9).

It is important to remember that children are not responsible for their family's problems. Although Sarah and Hagar were rivals and may have been enemies, their sons do not seem to have followed their behavior. We are responsible for how we treat other people, regardless of the situations we are in (Matthew 7:12; Philippians 2:3).

Family Flourish

The first meeting of Isaac and Rebekah reads like a fairy tale – it really was "love at first sight." As soon as they met, they married (Genesis 24:63-67). But their life together would not be easy. For 20 years, they faced the challenging stress of failure.

Almost every young married couple wants children, and it can be absolutely devastating when things do not work out. But most couples do not have to wait for 20 years. Isaac must have felt helpless. Rebekah may have felt that she was to blame. Yet once again, God rescued the man of faith.

> **We are responsible for how we treat other people, regardless of the situations we are in.**

Notice that Isaac turned to God in this moment of despair: "Isaac pleaded with the LORD for his wife," and she became pregnant (Genesis 25:21).

Repeated failures can either strengthen us to learn from mistakes and try even harder, or they can defeat us and cause us to give up. Isaac did not allow the stresses and problems of his life to destroy his spirit. Instead, he allowed stress to give birth to success by seeking refuge in God. Like Isaac, we should seek refuge in God. In the words of the psalmist, "Trust in Him at all times. … Pour out your heart before Him; God is a refuge for us" (Psalm 62:8).

Conclusion

Even though Isaac was born to fulfill the promise of God, his life was not free from anxiety and hurt. He faced family difficulty throughout his life, but he always looked to the Source of life for guidance and strength. He proved himself worthy of the promise by his righteous life. Some who read this book have had a relatively easy life; some have not. It is important for us to remember that all godly people will suffer difficulty in life (2 Timothy 3:12). Strangely, this is proof that the Lord, as a good Father, loves us (Hebrews 12:6). Even though Isaac was essential to the Lord's future plans for His people, God did not exempt him from stress and trouble. Why should we expect anything less for ourselves?

Discussion Questions

1. List three "firsts" in Isaac's life. In what ways do these "firsts" show the unfolding of God's plan?

2. List three exceptional qualities of Isaac's life. Do these make him more righteous than his father, Abraham, and his son Jacob?

3. Discuss the relationship of Sarah and Hagar. How might their conflicts have caused anxieties or stresses in Isaac's life?

4. Discuss the barrenness of Rebekah. How might the same problem today affect a married couple? How might a close relationship with God make a difference?

10

THE RISE
OF
RIGHTEOUS JACOB
Genesis 27-36

For some, doing the right thing just seems to come naturally. They do not seem to struggle with sin at all. Such spiritual giants might include our preachers, our elders, our parents or even our spouses. I once heard the wife of a faithful preacher claim that she had been spending the last 50 years trying to live up to her husband's example. Her adoration makes me think more of both him and her. At the same time, I have to wonder, "Does my life challenge others to become better?"

The Bible furnishes many examples of spiritual giants. One thinks of faithful women such as Esther or Ruth or of men such as Job or Daniel. These people seem to have found righteousness so easy. Even in the midst of great danger and persecution, they never seem to have lost focus. They remained humble and submissive to the will of God. So why is it that many of us find it so difficult to live Christian lives?

Why is it that many of us find it so difficult to live Christian lives?

Jacob must have asked himself similar questions. His grandfather, Abraham, was a spiritual giant. His father, Isaac, likewise justified the promise of God with his righteous life. But Jacob found it more difficult to be righteous. If we compare the "obituaries" of the three Patriarchs on the next page, we can clearly see the difference among the lives of Abraham, Isaac and Jacob.

Abraham

"Then Abraham breathed his last and died in a *good old age,* an old man and *full of years,* and was gathered to his people" (Genesis 25:8, emphasis added).

Isaac

"So Isaac breathed his last and died, and was gathered to his people, being *old* and *full of days.* And his sons Esau and Jacob buried him" (Genesis 35:29, emphasis added).

Jacob (to Pharoah)

"... *few and evil* have been the days of the years of my life, and *they have not attained to the days of the years of the life of my fathers* in the days of their pilgrimage" (Genesis 47:9, emphasis added).

Jacob himself acknowledged that his life had not been as long or as fulfilling as the lives of Abraham and Isaac. Perhaps the words of Job characterized the attitude of Jacob: "Man who is born of woman is of few days and full of trouble" (Job 14:1). But why did Jacob have such a hard life? Why did Jacob find spiritual success so difficult?

The Struggles of Jacob

In the year 1993, the rock group R.E.M. released a popular single titled "Everybody Hurts." The melancholy music and lyrics strike a chord with those feeling worthless and helpless. The challenges that life often hurls against us seem so suffocating at times. Yet we understand that persecution is promised (2 Timothy 3:12). We know that suffering provides an opportunity to imitate the example of Christ (1 Peter 2:20-21). Whether we face emotional or physical difficulty, our struggles serve to focus our perspective. Paul petitioned the Lord on three occasions to remove his "thorn in the flesh," and each time received the response: "My grace is sufficient for you, for My strength is made perfect in weakness" (2 Corinthians 12:8-9). The strength of God is at its strongest when we are at our weakest. Jacob was forced through both emotional and physical challenges to overcome trust in self and to place his trust in God.

Overcoming Selfishness

Jacob's name means "supplanter." The name indicates that Jacob succeeded only at the expense of others. Early in his life, we see his tendencies at work – first when he tricked his hungry brother, Esau, into sacrificing his birthright for a bowl of soup (Genesis 25:29-34). Jacob obtained what he wanted at the expense of someone else. Then, at the instigation of his mother, Jacob robbed Esau of his father's blessing, which only the firstborn son should have received (27:1-41). Jacob had become an expert in swindling others; he had become an expert in selfishness.

> **Selfishness is an epidemic in our world. We witness far more prodigal sons than forgiving fathers.**

Selfishness is an epidemic in our world. We witness far more prodigal sons than forgiving fathers (cf. Luke 15:11-32). "Do whatever it takes." "Backstab, cheat and mistreat whomever you need to in order to get what you want." "Look out for numero uno." These ideas may prevail in our modern culture, and they may be exhibited in Jacob's early life. But they are not godly ideas.

Paul challenged: "Let nothing be done through selfish ambition or conceit, but in lowliness of mind let each esteem others better than himself. Let each of you look out not only for his own interests, but also for the interests of others" (Philippians 2:3-4). We must never belittle another in order to better ourselves. Selfishness has no place in the life of a Christian (2 Corinthians 12:20; Galatians 5:20). Our work as Christians means that we must seek to build up, not to tear down. The Bible describes this as "edification." Paul commanded, "Let each of us please his neighbor for his good, leading to edification" (Romans 15:2). The apostles did everything they could to edify the church (2 Corinthians 12:19). Selfishness causes us to treat others as tools to get what we want; it blinds us to the needs and feelings of others and leaves us with few friends and many social casualties. Jacob had to overcome selfishness on his path to godliness.

Overcoming Spiritual Weakness

On a number of occasions, Jacob appeared spiritually weak. He appeared morally weak when he allowed his mother to talk him into deceiving his aged father (Genesis 27:1-41). He appeared idolatrous when he constructed and anointed a "pillar" in honor of God – an act later prohibited (28:18; 35:14; cf. Leviticus 26:1; Deuteronomy 16:22). He appeared religiously ignorant when he offered to God his allegiance in exchange for a safe passage back to Canaan (Genesis 28:20-22). He appeared foolish when he believed that he had "seen God face to face" (32:30). He appeared insensitive when he ranked his family in order of the value of their lives (33:2). He appeared unfair when he substituted Ephraim for Manasseh as firstborn of Joseph (48:17-20).

Despite his spiritual struggles, God never lost faith in Jacob.

None of these qualities is admirable. It goes without saying that Jacob had lots of room for improvement. Nevertheless, despite his spiritual struggles, God never lost faith in Jacob. He continued to bless Jacob both with family and finances (Genesis 29:32–30:24, 43; 31:1). He continued to hold true to the promise He had given to Abraham and Isaac. It is intriguing that of the three Patriarchs, Jacob was blessed with a larger family than Abraham and Isaac combined.

God wants us to aim for perfection (Matthew 5:48; James 1:4), but He recognizes that humans make mistakes (Romans 3:10, 12, 23). We often "miss the mark" – the very definition of the Greek term for "sin." Some biblical characters commit really major sins against God. David was an adulterer and a murderer (2 Samuel 11), but he repented of his sin (Psalm 51). King Manasseh of Judah was one of the most wicked men in the Old Testament, but he offered a prayer of repentance, which the Lord heard and accepted (2 Chronicles 33:12-19). Although we may not be adulterous murderers like David or may not finance the building of structures to worship other gods like Manasseh, we are all guilty – just as they were – of sinning against the Lord. If the Lord forgave and blessed these great Old Testament characters, how much more will He forgive and bless us?

Overcoming Fear

President Franklin Delano Roosevelt once delivered a speech in which he emphatically declared, "The only thing we have to fear is fear itself." The same can be said about worry. I once heard someone say, "About 80 percent of everything we worry about never actually happens." Human beings can reach the point of fear, which leads to worry, to stress, to poor health and to a lower quality of life. Jacob knew about fear and worry.

We are told in the Scriptures that Jacob fled his home because Esau was plotting to kill him (Genesis 27:41-43). Jacob had been away from home for more than 20 years when he finally returned to Canaan (31:38, 41). Just prior to his entrance, he was informed, "We came to your brother Esau, and he also is coming to meet you, and four hundred men are with him" (32:6). Why did Esau need such a large force? Was he planning to murder Jacob and his entire family?

The Bible reports that Jacob was "greatly afraid and distressed" (Genesis 32:7). He worried and obsessed over his fear. He divided his camp, went away alone, and even wrestled with an "Angel" all night (cf. Hosea 12:4). Yet the reunion between Jacob and Esau was not an occasion of bloodshed but one of brotherhood. In language reminiscent of the forgiving father in the parable of the prodigal son, the Bible beautifully reports, "Esau ran to meet [Jacob], and embraced him, and fell on his neck and kissed him, and they wept" (Genesis 33:4; cf. Luke 15:20).

It can sometimes take a tremendous amount of willpower to overcome fear. Whether the occasion involves accepting an invitation to teach a public class or confronting someone about a personal problem, fear and worry can take their toll. Let us remember the words of the psalmist: "The LORD is on my side; I will not fear. What can man do to me?" (Psalm 118:6).

Conclusion

One of the most valuable pieces of advice I have ever received is this: "Don't put people in a box." This advice reminds me that people can change. Young women who appear selfish and vain as teenagers can grow to serve and love others just a few years later. Young men who tend to be egotistical in their 20s can become sacrificial and deferential in their 30s. Do not judge people at an early age! Don't put someone in a box without allowing him room to grow.

If we try to judge Jacob by the behavior he demonstrated as a youth, we might come away thinking he was a failure. He was nothing more than a liar or a cheat ... and maybe a momma's boy. But God refused to give up on Jacob. Although Jacob continued to make mistakes, as we all do, he was ultimately successful in transferring the promise of God to the next generation.

Righteousness comes easy for no one. But righteousness will prove even more challenging if we, like Jacob, continually make decisions that put our righteousness at risk. We should avoid situations in which it becomes very difficult to make good decisions and remain faithful to God. For example, if I struggle with the sin of lust (Matthew 5:28), I should avoid parties where people are dressed immodestly.

> **Don't put someone in a box without allowing him room to grow.**

If I want to avoid using filthy language (Colossians 3:8), I should probably avoid those who use it themselves. Christians must keep themselves pure from corrupting influences (2 Corinthians 6:17). If we, like Jacob, can persevere through temptation, we too will be judged as faithful (Hebrews 11:21).

Discussion Questions

1. Why do you think some people appear more righteous than others? Do you think righteousness comes easier to some than others?

2. Briefly compare the lives of Abraham, Isaac and Jacob.

What mistakes did they make? How did they respond to those mistakes?

3. Discuss different ways selfishness is present in our world. How does selfishness affect our relationships?

4. How does fear affect our lives? Can fear be a good thing? When does fear become destructive?

11

COPING WITH
REJECTION:
JOSEPH IN CANAAN
Genesis 37

Eric Harris, Dylan Klebold, Charles Andrew Williams, Jeff Weise – all these teens have one thing in common: They opened fire on teachers and classmates in their schools. In the area where I am from in western Kentucky, a student named Michael Carneal opened fire on a prayer circle in December 1997, killing three and wounding five more. He was only 14 years old at the time.

What makes young people commit such crimes? What motivates someone to feel that life is so hopeless that it would be more satisfying to kill than to coexist? In the investigations that followed each of these shootings, one finding emerges time and again: These young men felt as if they didn't belong. They weren't popular. They tended to be loners. Other people just tended to ignore them.

> Maybe you have felt it is safer to stay quiet and keep to yourself than to risk being ridiculed.

Maybe you have felt the same way. Maybe you have felt ignored. Maybe you have felt it is safer to stay quiet and keep to yourself than to risk being ridiculed. Sometimes it seems that other people just don't care. I wonder how many of those shooting tragedies could have been avoided if just one person had taken an interest in those young men. What if they had just one friend to encourage them and make them feel important?

To Be Godly Is to Be Different

If you feel as if you don't belong, read the Bible. Many biblical characters felt exactly the same way. Moses must have appeared insane when he left a princely lifestyle in Egypt "to suffer affliction with the people of God" (Hebrews 11:25). Joshua and Caleb were nearly killed because they stood alone against the majority (Numbers 14:10). Elijah felt that he was isolated (1 Kings 18:22; 19:10, 14). Jeremiah was often rejected and ignored (e.g., Jeremiah 26, 38). And let us not forget that Jesus Christ was executed on a cross!

Living godly lives will always make us different. Rarely in the Bible do we see the majority of people faithfully submitting to God. Jesus stated that many will go to destruction, but few will enter life (Matthew 7:13-14). So God's people are always in the minority. They are always to be different from others in the world. We can even expect to be hated (John 15:19; 17:14). But we must remain faithful (Revelation 2:10).

God's people are always to be different from others in the world.

Although we may feel isolated and ignored from time to time, we do not live for ourselves but for the Lord Jesus (1 Corinthians 6:20). Our upward focus keeps everything else in perspective (Colossians 3:1-2).

Joseph experienced some ups and downs in his life, but he never seems to have lost his perspective. He did not derive his sense of self-worth from other people. Whether he was hated or adored, he remained equally committed to the Lord. This first lesson on Joseph focuses on his early life as a marginalized member of his own family. What did he do when hardly anyone cared about him?

Joseph Was Different

Joseph was unique, although not always by choice. He was often isolated from his family by circumstances beyond his control. He was the older son of his father's deceased wife, Rachel, who was also his father's favorite wife (Genesis 29:30). Because of this, Joseph's father, Jacob, "loved Joseph more than all his children" (37:3). This parental preference caused Joseph's 10 older brothers to dislike him, and when Joseph received a special coat from his father, he was further alienated from them (vv. 3-4).

Joseph was also different because he was a dreamer. His dreams were from the Lord, and he chose to share them with his brothers (Genesis 37:5). In these dreams, Joseph was placed above both his brothers and his parents (vv. 7-10). Because Joseph lived in a strictly hierarchal family unit where the 11th-born son ranked very low on the scale of importance, his dreams were an insult.

Unless Joseph was completely clueless, he must have known how his brothers felt about him. He must have felt isolated and unimportant. But he was a young man of integrity. Notice that he was willing to bring a bad report about his brothers to his father (Genesis 37:2). Although we cannot say for certain what his brothers were doing wrong, Joseph felt that their offenses were serious enough to be reported.

Some people turn a blind eye to sin. They learn that a colleague is involved in an extra-marital affair or that their superiors are intentionally mismanaging company funds, but instead of reporting the offenses, they shrink back out of fear. They don't want to be viewed as a tattletale. They don't want to alienate themselves from others. They don't want to be at the center of the controversy.

We must be committed to godliness no matter the consequences.

Joseph was not concerned about that. He did the right thing because it was the right thing to do. Like Joseph, we must be committed to godliness no matter the consequences. We do not become godly in the midst of crisis. We determine to be godly before the crisis arises.

The Consequences of Being Different

It's okay to be different, as long as we are different for the right reasons. Purple suits and nose piercings may cause people to *look* unique, but these things do not *make* them unique. Uniqueness comes from our character. We know that pursuing a godly character will automatically mark us as unique, but we need to realize that godliness will also bring persecution (Matthew 5:10). Joseph's unique, godly nature cost him everything.

The brothers of Joseph conspired to kill him (Genesis 37:20). Only the greed of Joseph's brothers saved his life. They sold him as a slave to traders passing through the region (v. 28). Joseph's faithfulness to God almost cost him his life.

Others have lost their lives because of godly living. Think of Isaiah, who, according to tradition, was sawn in two (cf. Hebrews 11:37). Think of Zechariah, who was stoned (2 Chronicles 24:21). Think of John, who was beheaded (Mark 6:27). Think of Jesus, who was crucified (15:25). All these men were innocent, but they were killed because they stood for the truth.

Joseph, likewise, did nothing to deserve the treatment he received, but he received it because he was different from his brothers. If you wish to be godly, expect to be different. Expect to be persecuted. But also expect to be rewarded (1 Peter 5:10).

The Christian's Self-Worth

Christians should not derive their sense of self-worth from other people. If you are a Christian, you should be proud of who you are and where you are going. You are a citizen of a "kingdom ... not of this world" (John 18:36). Your "citizenship is in heaven" (Philippians 3:20). Whatever others say, think or post on Facebook cannot shake our confidence. All these things belong to a world that is temporary (2 Corinthians 4:17-18). They do not matter. Have the courage to be different. God loves you. He doesn't just *like* you. He *loves* you – so much so that He sent His Son to die for you (2 Corinthians 5:15). Being unique is simply to follow in the footsteps of the Savior. The Jewish leaders thought Jesus had a demon (John 10:20). The governor Festus thought Paul was crazy (Acts 26:24). But Jesus and Paul did not change their view of themselves based on what others thought. They recognized their role in God's kingdom. The Christian's sense of self-worth is based on God's love and promise of reward (Colossians 3:24).

> **The Christian's sense of self-worth is based on God's love and promise of reward.**

Conclusion

I was a counselor at a summer Bible camp for several years. One year, I had a camper who was particularly memorable. At lunch one day he noticed another boy sitting alone with his meal. He asked me, "Is he all by himself?"

"It appears that way," I responded.

Soon the lone camper was surrounded by about 12 other boys. His spirits were immediately lifted. As Christians we often feel alone. Like Elijah, we may believe that everyone has forsaken the Lord, and we alone are left (1 Kings 19:10). But there is usually a team of Christians willing and able to surround us and lift us up.

We must run away from the devil and rush toward Christ and His church.

We cannot please all the people all the time. If we try, we will be left ruining our lives and disappointing others. We must live for the Master. We must be unique. We must run away from the devil and rush toward Christ and His church (James 4:7-8). We must take a stand against ungodly behavior in every form. In so doing, we will be mocked, excluded and labeled. So what? As Christ challenged, "Rejoice and be exceedingly glad, for great is your reward in heaven, for so they persecuted the prophets who were before you" (Matthew 5:12).

Joseph stood out because of his character. Joseph stood out because of his father's preference. Joseph stood out because of his spiritual gift of prophetic dreams. Yet he never compromised his integrity or apologized for telling the truth. Our Christian character may lead us to stand out. Others may misunderstand us or ridicule us. Like Joseph, we all today must accept persecution while maintaining an unshakable confidence in our reward (2 Corinthians 1:7).

Discussion Questions

1. When is being different a bad thing? When is being different a good thing?

2. List some ways Christians should be different from others.

3. How was Joseph different from his brothers? How can we become less like the brothers and more like Joseph?

4. What are the dangers of deriving your sense of self-worth from other people?

5. God loves you and gave His Son for you. How does this fact change the way we ought to live?

12

COPING WITH
FAME:
JOSEPH IN EGYPT
Genesis 39-48

Most people in the U.S. are unhappy with their jobs. According to a 2012 survey from Right Management, 65 percent of Americans are unhappy with their jobs.[1] I think this is because many people choose to follow a worldly definition of success.

I remember telling my aunt how long it would take me to earn my doctorate. When she learned I would be in college for approximately 12 years, she exclaimed, "In that amount of time, you could be a *real* doctor!" Although a Ph.D. in religious studies meant much to me, my aunt defined success differently. Being a surgeon or a medical doctor represented success to her. Being a college professor did not.

> "Trust in the LORD with all your heart, and lean not on your own understanding" (Proverbs 3:5).

It is important for Christians to remain true to God's definition of success instead of allowing another person's definition to alter their course. The only way to be truly successful is to "trust in the LORD with all your heart, and lean not on your own understanding" (Proverbs 3:5). If we put God first, everything else will fall into place (Matthew 6:33).

The Success of Joseph

Joseph would have been considered successful by any definition of success. Whereas he had been marginalized and mistreated by his own family, he became a "rock star" in Egypt. It took a few years for Joseph's prominence to peak, but he had success from the moment he entered Egypt. The Bible tells us why: "The LORD was with Joseph, and he was a successful man" (Genesis 39:2). A clearer translation is provided by the New American Standard Bible: "The LORD was with Joseph, *so* he became a successful man" (emphasis added). The Lord was and is the only reason for true success. Yet Joseph's life was not always smooth sailing; he encountered difficulties and temptations. Being successful is no guarantee against affliction.

While all of us want to be successful, it is tempting to allow ourselves to become so myopic that we are blinded to the temptations that can accompany success.

Success Comes With Attractions

One celebrity musician requests dressing rooms only with white furniture. Another demands bowls filled only with blue M&M's. Many celebrities allow their fame and for-

> **Success is no guarantee against affliction.**

tune to go to their heads; they ignore their fans and mistreat their friends. They allow the attractions of their status to change who they are. But when their star burns out and their celebrity status fades, they soon find that their abuse of others has led to resentment. Unlike most celebrities, Joseph never forgot where he came from. When everyone began to like him, he remained the same as when no one had liked him.

Joseph was about 17 years old when he entered Egypt. At that age, it would have been easy to fall victim to all the attractions that accompany success, and Joseph had plenty of opportunities. The Bible records that Potiphar "made [Joseph] overseer of his house, and all that he had he put under his authority" (Genesis 39:4). Joseph was in a position to embezzle money, to live luxuriously, and to take advantage of everything success had to offer. But he placed limits on himself.

When the wife of Potiphar proposed a sexual relationship, Joseph refused (Genesis 39:7-9). Joseph had ample opportunity to reconsider, for she approached him "day by day" (v. 10). Notice how Joseph responded. First, he remembered God (v. 9). Not only would a sexual encounter have violated his master's trust, but it also would have violated *the* Master's trust. Joseph refused to jeopardize his relationship with the Lord. Second, he responded clearly (v. 9). Although Potiphar's wife was an influential woman, he chastised her for proposing "great wickedness." Joseph made sure she knew exactly how he felt about her offer. Third, he was resolute. Temptations often grow more attractive when we face them every day, but Joseph never waned in his firmness and godly conviction.

> **Temptations often grow more attractive when we face them every day, but Joseph never waned in his firmness and godly conviction.**

The attraction of a sexual relationship with an older, probably attractive woman would likely cause most teenagers and many middle-aged adults to fall. Not Joseph. He proved himself faithful both to his master and to God. But he was not rewarded. After Potiphar's wife tearfully accused Joseph of rape, he was thrown into prison for two years (Genesis 39:11-20). Joseph had experienced enough "bad luck" for a lifetime, and he was not yet 20 years old! Nevertheless, "the LORD was with Joseph and showed him mercy, and He gave him favor in the sight of the keeper of the prison" (v. 21).

Success Comes With Opportunities

Although Joseph was innocent, he sat as a criminal in prison. Some might not see this chapter in the life of Joseph as a success, but it was. He was suffering for doing good (1 Peter 2:20). Joseph himself never blamed God for his plight. In fact, rather than viewing prison as an affliction, Joseph used prison as an opportunity. Joseph never could have risen above the level of a slave if he had not been thrown into prison. His suffering made him successful.

Joseph was successful almost immediately after his incarceration. The Bible records: "The keeper of the prison did not look into anything that was under Joseph's authority, because the LORD was with him; and whatever he did, the LORD made it prosper" (Genesis 39:23). Again, we can see the Lord's activity in the life of Joseph.

Soon after Joseph's imprisonment, Pharaoh's chief butler and chief baker were also thrown into prison (Genesis 40:2-3). We learned earlier

True success is measured in terms of service to God. in Joseph's life that he was a dreamer (37:5-9). Now we learn that Joseph also had the gift of dream interpretation (40:12-13, 18-19). The chief butler was restored, and the chief baker, executed, just as Joseph had predicted (vv. 21-22). Although not immediately, this prediction led to the opportunity for Joseph to correctly interpret Pharaoh's dream, which led to Joseph becoming Pharaoh's right-hand man. Wherever he went and whatever he did, Joseph was successful!

Success Comes With Rewards

True success is measured in terms of service to God (cf. Joshua 1:8). Joseph's unwavering commitment to the Lord led him out of prison into the courts of Pharaoh. After Joseph successfully interpreted Pharaoh's perplexing dream about seven cows and seven ears of grain, he was brought from prison and assigned by Pharaoh a series of honors:

- Joseph was placed over all of Egypt (Genesis 41:41).

- Joseph received Pharaoh's signet ring (v. 42).

- Joseph received expensive royal clothing and jewelry (v. 42).

- Joseph rode in the second chariot (v. 43).

- Joseph received an Egyptian name (v. 45).

- Joseph received Asenath, the daughter of an Egyptian priest, as his wife (v. 45).

Perhaps the attitude of Pharaoh toward Joseph can be best summarized with the following: "I am Pharaoh, and without your consent no man may lift his hand or foot in all the land of Egypt" (v. 44).

Joseph achieved great success, and he did not need to sacrifice his godliness in order to do so. Too many people today believe they must jettison their Christian morality in order to be accepted and respected by others. Joseph remained faithful to God no matter where that led. And wherever he went, others were made better because of his presence. Can we say the same of ourselves?

Conclusion

Modern American culture has decided that no one ought to suffer. Parents should not discipline their children; teachers should not give F's; and everyone equally deserves the best of everything. But suffering can bring about positive results. In Joseph's life, we witness much that was unfair, yet Joseph did not whine about mistreatment. He remained faithful to God. Like Paul, Joseph learned to be content in every place and circumstance (Philippians 4:11). Unlike the Pharisees, Joseph re-

Fear God and keep His commandments, for this is man's all

solved to practice what he preached (Matthew 23:3). And despite his suffering and his condition, people liked Joseph everywhere he went.

People didn't like Joseph because he was successful. Rather, his commitment to God made him stand out among others. People recognized his gifts and assigned him positions of prominence.

What do you do when everyone likes you? The same things you do when no one likes you. "Let us hear the conclusion of the whole matter: Fear God and keep His commandments, for this is man's all. For God will bring every work into judgment, including every secret thing, whether good or evil" (Ecclesiastes 12:13-14).

Discussion Questions

1. How does modern culture define success? How does this definition differ from the biblical definition of success?

2. List three goals you hope to achieve within the next 10 years. How does God fit into those goals?

3. Why was Joseph successful? How can we find the kind of success Joseph experienced?

4. Joseph was a foreign ex-convict and former slave who worshiped a God different from that of any of the Egyptian people. Yet he was still liked and appreciated. Why? Can we as Christians be different from everyone around us and still be liked and appreciated?

13

BLESSINGS
FROM A
DYING FATHER
Genesis 48-50

D eathbed statements are always powerful. Sometimes they are
negative, such as Italian artist Leonardo da Vinci's "I have offended God and mankind because my work did not reach the quality it
should have." Sometimes they are positive, such as American inventor
Thomas Edison's "It is very beautiful over there." Sometimes they
are comical, such as the Roman emperor Vespasian's "Woe is me. Me
thinks I'm turning into a god," referring to the tendency of the Roman senate to "make" dead emperors into gods.[1] However, the most
compelling last words were spoken by the Lord when He quoted Psalm
31:5: "Father, into Your hands I commit My spirit" (Luke 23:46).

In the world of the Old Testament, deathbed statements were often
viewed as important events. It was believed that the individual was
expressing his deepest desires. Isaac wished to bless Esau because, as he
stated, "I am old. I do not know the day of my death" (Genesis 27:2).
Apparently, Isaac believed his death was imminent. Certainly there was
an enduring, irrevocable quality to the words spoken on this occasion
(vv. 30-38). Partially because of Isaac's blessing of Jacob, God later
extended the promise of Abraham and Isaac to Jacob (28:13-15). Just
as with Isaac's words uttered in old age, the last words of Jacob were
expected to reflect important lessons about the future of his children.

The Power of Memory

Imagine how Joseph must have felt when he was sold to the Ishmaelites

Memories are powerful tools. (Genesis 37:28). He must have been sure he would never see his father again. The memories of his childhood, of his father's love, and even of his deceased mother must have filled his heart with sadness. Still, Joseph's memories of home must have consoled him during those dark hours in an Egyptian prison.

Memories are powerful tools. They encourage us to repeat good behaviors and warn us to avoid bad ones. They form who we will be and challenge us to become better. The memories of youth are especially powerful to us. In the words of Thomas Moore's "Oft in the Stilly Night,"

> Oft in the stilly night,
> Ere slumber's chain has bound me,
> Fond Memory brings the light
> Of other days around me:
> The smiles, the tears
> Of boyhood's years,
> The words of love then spoken;
> The eyes that shone,
> Now dimmed and gone,
> The cheerful hearts now broken.[2]

It is important to remember our past. Every family vacation, every fatherly conversation, every motherly embrace, every brotherly piece of advice, every sisterly tear should register in our minds like an entry in the book of our lives. Yet in order to have memories later in life, we must take the time to make them in the here and now. Joseph, like the prodigal son, must have cherished every memory he had of home when he was in a faraway land (cf. Luke 15:17). He must have thought often of his family and wondered what had become of his father. Little did he know that, after a gap of more than 20 years, they would be reunited.

Caring for Aged Parents

Memories become even more important as our parents reach the end of their lives. People often regret things in old age, but I have never heard anyone say they regretted the time they spent with their parents. For some reason, we often fail to realize how special they are until they get older. It is at least safe to say most young people think their parents are out of touch. In fact, sociologists find that we often identify much more closely with our grandparents than we do with our parents. Still, our parents deserve our time, respect and obedience.

Although we often apply the verse to teenagers exclusively, there is no biblical time limit on the words "honor your father and your mother" (Exodus 20:12; Deuteronomy 5:16). Indeed, some scholars believe the most logical application of this command in ancient Israel would have been in taking care of aged parents. We should **Parents deserve our time, respect and obedience** honor our parents, especially if they are older. If we fail to make time for our parents now, we might look up one day to notice they are gone.

When Joseph learned that his father was ill, he immediately went to Jacob along with his sons (Genesis 48:1). Jacob expressed sadness over the death of Joseph's mother, Rachel (v. 7). But the penetrating statement comes several verses later: "And Israel said to Joseph, 'I had not thought to see your face; but in fact, God has also shown me your offspring!' " (v. 11).

Jacob had believed Joseph to be dead (Genesis 37:34-35). He must have remembered Joseph as a boy and as a teenager. He must have regretted the decision to send Joseph to his brothers (v. 14). He must have wondered whether Joseph put up a fight when the wild beasts tore apart his body (v. 33). But all the bad memories faded away with the news of Joseph's existence and success (45:26). Joy was brought to a dying father by the presence of a faithful son.

Final Words of a Dying Father

The Bible takes two chapters to record the death of Jacob (Genesis 48–49). The majority of those chapters is spent detailing the words Jacob spoke to his sons. Jacob had his struggles in life, but he found the strength to address each of his sons in the moments leading to his death. At this point, the promise of God passed on to the nation of Israel. Thus, the dying words of Jacob became foundational for the fortunes of his people.

Passing the Torch

One of the great traditions of the Olympics is the passing of the torch. For months, athletes transfer the torch from one city to another until it finally lights the massive Olympic torch at the center of the host city's stadium. In a similar way, every father wishes to pass on part of himself to his children. Especially in older age, a father thinks about what he will leave behind – not only in terms of material possessions but also in terms of values and memories.

Jacob passed the torch of leadership to Ephraim and Manasseh, the sons of Joseph (Genesis 48:14). In later history, we learn the tribes of Ephraim and Manasseh were distinguished for their numbers and their faithfulness.

Every father wishes to pass on part of himself to his children.

Ephraim produced 40,500 men of war when Israel left Egypt (Numbers 1:33). Hoshea son of Nun, whose name was changed by Moses to Joshua, was from the tribe of Ephraim (13:8, 16). Manasseh was also distinguished in number (Deuteronomy 33:17). Indeed, by the time of the second census, Manasseh's numbers had increased to 52,700 (Numbers 26:34). Gideon was from the territory of Manasseh, securing an honored place for this tribe in Israel's military history.

Professing the Truth

Fathers tend to view their children through rose-colored glasses. They often fail to see the faults of their children and grandchildren. Jacob, however, experienced an unusually clear-minded judgment. He recognized that some of his sons would be distinguished while others would be disqualified. Among those who received negative professions were Reuben (Genesis 49:3-4), Simeon and Levi (vv. 5-7). The disqualification of these firstborn sons by Jacob is usually understood to have paved the way for the prominence of Judah in later history (vv. 8-12). But it is also true that these sons disqualified themselves by their own actions.

Reuben slept with his father's concubine Bilhah (Genesis 35:22). Because Bilhah was the servant of Rachel, she must have been very dear to Jacob. This disgraceful sexual encounter disqualified the natural firstborn son, Reuben. Simeon and Levi were disqualified by their anger over the rape of Dinah, their sister. Although Shechem violated Dinah, he wished to marry her, and Jacob arranged the marriage. But Simeon and Levi went against their father's wishes, murdered Shechem and his people, and retrieved their sister from the home of her new husband (34:25-31).

We cannot conclude from these accounts that the descendants of these sons would have been evil. In fact, the Levites went on to be the priests of God. Every individual must answer for himself. Ezekiel said: "The soul who sins shall die. The

Ultimately we are responsible for our own actions.

son shall not bear the guilt of the father, nor the father bear the guilt of the son. The righteousness of the righteous shall be upon himself, and the wickedness of the wicked shall be upon himself" (Ezekiel 18:20). Although our parents attempt to point us in the right direction, ultimately we are responsible for our own actions. And like Reuben, Simeon and Levi, we will have to pay the consequences. How will we live?

Conclusion

Jacob was not always a great father. The favoritism he showed Joseph certainly did not encourage his other sons. Yet the Bible still asks us to be respectful toward our parents no matter what choices they make. It should be our aim to love, honor and respect our parents, even when we disagree with them. Jonathan certainly did not want his father to kill David, but he had the respect to talk to Saul about it. He at least tried to work out a solution, even if the solution failed (cf. 1 Samuel 19). In most cases, our parents love us and want the best for us, but even if that is not true with our parents, it is true with God. So let us serve Him. Let us love Him. He has promised, "I will not leave you nor forsake you" (Joshua 1:5; cf. Hebrews 13:5).

Discussion Questions

1. If you could choose your last words now, which would you choose? Why?

2. It is much easier to honor someone who is honorable. How can we develop better relationships both with our children and with our parents to promote the honor God intended?

3. Why is it important to store up and reflect on our memories? Why is it also important to live in the present? How do you find the balance between the two?

4. If a person has negligent, absent or perhaps abusive parents, should that person still seek to honor his or her parents? If yes, then how?

Endnotes

Lesson 1

1 The full quote runs as follows: "After Buddha was dead, they still showed his shadow in a cave for centuries – a tremendous gruesome shadow. God is dead; but given the way people are, there may still for millennia be caves in which they show his shadow. And we – we must still defeat his shadow as well!" Friedrich Nietzsche, *The Gay Science*, Book III, 108 (trans. Josefine Nauckhoff, Cambridge Texts in the History of Philosophy. Cambridge: Cambridge University Press, 2001, p. 109).

2 The point about rocks and dirt producing life is borrowed from Antony G.N. Flew and Thomas B. Warren, *The Warren-Flew Debate on the Existence of God* (Jonesboro: National Christian Press, 1977).

Lesson 4

1 See Targum Pseudo-Jonathan and Targum Neofiti on Genesis 3:15 for examples of a Messianic Jewish reading. See Irenaeus, *Against All Heresies* 5.21.1-2, and Cyprian, *To Quirinus* 2.9, for examples of a Christian Messianic reading.

Lesson 5

1 For more information, see http://www.covenanteyes.com/2010/08/19/teens-and-porn-10-stats-your-need-to-know/.

Lesson 6

1 See www.cdc.gov/alcohol/fact-sheets/alcohol-use.htm.

2 See http://www.indepthprogram.com/Cocaine.html.

3 See www.cdc.gov/motorvehiclesafety/impaired_driving/impaired-drv-fact-sheet.html.

4 See www.cdc.gov/alcohol/fact-sheets/alcohol-use.htm.

5 See http://www.ncadd.org/index.php/learn-about-alcohol/alcohol-and-crime.

6 http://pubs.niaaa.nih.gov/publications/UnderageDrinking/Underage_Fact.pdf.

7 Homer, *Odyssey* 9.208-09.

8 Pliny, *Natural History* 14.6.54.

9 Robert H. Stein, "Wine-Drinking in New Testament Times," *Christianity Today* 19 (June 20, 1975) 11.

Lesson 7

1 Qtd. in Nahum Sarna, *Understanding Genesis* (New York: Schoken, 1966) 67.

2 James Pritchard, ed., *Ancient Near Eastern Texts Relating to the Old Testament* (Princeton: Princeton University Press, 1950) 270.

Lesson 8

1 For an example, see Pritchard 220.

Lesson 9

1 www.ourbabynamer.com/Isaac-name-popularity.html

2 See A.B. Luter and S.L. Klouda, "Isaac," *Dictionary of the Old Testament Pentateuch*, eds. T. Desmond Alexander and David W. Baker (Downers Grove: IVP, 2003).

Lesson 12

1 See http://www.forbes.com/sites/susanadams/2012/05/18/new-survey-majority-of-employees-dissatisfied/.

Lesson 13

1 A number of websites report the alleged last words of famous people. The one I have used is http://corsinet.com/braincandy/dying.html.

2 See http://www.bartleby.com/360/6/143.html.

CPSIA information can be obtained at www.ICGtesting.com
Printed in the USA
LVOW05s0343101014

408179LV00002B/2/P